HIS BRIDE HAS MADE HERSELF READY

FOR THOSE WHO YEARN TO FULFILL THE PASSIONATE DESIRE OF THE BRIDEGROOM'S HEART.

DEBRA WEBSTER

Published by His Glory Publishing
P.O. Box 20296
Indianapolis, IN 46220-0296
bridegroomsglory.com

Acknowledgements

George, without you none this is possible.

Dedication

This book is dedicated to the bride within the church waiting in the secret place listening for the sound of his voice.

TABLE OF CONTENTS

PREFACE

PART ONE-THE PROBLEM

PART TWO-THE SOLUTIONS

Preface

Church leaders and lay people alike believe we are living in the last of the Last Days. The scriptures tell us, "His bride has made herself ready." (Rev. 19:7) This passage contains Last Day's prophecy from the book of Revelation. So, history's culmination will include a bride ready for her Holy Husband. What does it mean for the bride to be ready?

First, we must understand that the book of Revelation is the "Revelation of Jesus Christ". Revelation is more than his revelation. It is a book revealing the bride of his heart as well. In the closing chapters of Revelation, we see the bride. Before he introduces the bride again, he judges the harlot. The harlot is the counterfeit bride.

After judging the harlot an angel who took part in the bowl judgments introduces the bride. This is beyond significant. Jesus Christ's revelation of his triumph over everything false includes the bride. This underlines what scripture tells us. History is his story. Because history is his story, and he chose us, it includes his bride.

When God judges the Harlot and she no longer can manipulate and control, the bride company is shown as complete. Since the wheat and tares grow together, this makes sense.

John 1 tells us that our Savior made the world. This passage calls Jesus both the Word of God and the Lamb of God. Throughout the scriptures, God calls his people many things. Among them are sheep, my people, children of God, adopted sons and so forth. At the end of history Rev. 21 calls the people of God His bride, the wife of the Lamb and the New Jerusalem (Rev. 19-21).

Before the Word of God created the heavens, earth and man, God desired fellowship with man such as that which the Godhead enjoys. The Word created Adam and Eve and marriage to show us the fellowship that exists between Christ, his Father and the Holy Spirit and that he desires with us. He wrote a book of the bible to illustrate his intention to us. Song of Songs is more than a biblical book. It contains the song above every other song. It is the song the Bridegroom Lamb has been singing over his Bride since before he created us. From Genesis 3 when the voice of God walked in the garden with Adam and Eve until the end of Revelation the theme of intimate communion is the theme above every other theme. So, the end of time in Rev. 19-21 centers on the fulfillment of the Bridegroom's love because that was his eternal intention in creation.

Rev. 21:9. 'One of the seven angels who had the seven bowls full of the seven last plagues came and said to me, "Come, I will show you the bride, the wife of the Lamb." 10. And he carried me away in the Spirit to a mountain great and high, and showed me the Holy City, Jerusalem, coming down out of heaven from God.'

Regarding this city, we are told in Rev. 21:22. "And I saw no temple in it, for the Lord God, the Almighty, and the Lamb, are its temple. 23. The city does not need the sun or the moon to shine on it, for the glory of God gives it light, and the Lamb is its lamp."

Within this city is the Lord God Almighty and the Lamb as both the temple and the light of the city. The total fulfillment of God's presence the bride has yearned for is within this bride city. God created us to become this city.

Building large ministries that appear successful or accumulating the world's goods are not important. Also, not important is doing good works to help us impress others. In fact, we must get ready and disciple others so they might get ready. Readiness may include a large ministry, financial provision and good works, but that must not be the focus. If the Lord is truly our eternal focus, then we must focus on the Bridegroom himself now if we are to be ready.

It is easy to lose focus. The early church did. What can we learn from them and how can we make ourselves ready? This book is not an exhaustive study of this question but, examines a portion of what it takes to get ready.

CHAPTER 1
THE PROBLEM OF GETTING READY

Rev. 19:6 "Hallelujah! For the Lord our God, the Almighty, reigns. 7. Let us rejoice and be glad and give the glory to Him, for the marriage of the Lamb has come and His bride has made herself ready."

Most of us are familiar with the biblical statement "His bride has made herself ready." But what does that mean? According to this passage, she is ready for the Lamb's wedding and she is his bride. How has she "made herself ready"? Verse 8 gives us clues. 8. "It was given to her to clothe herself in fine linen, bright and clean; for the fine linen is the righteous acts of the saints." His bride is given fine linen to wear. The bride receiving this to wear will become significant in a later chapter. This fine linen is the righteous acts she does. These righteous acts are obedient actions in response to his voice. We will examine obedient response to his voice in later chapters as well. Both subjects are critically important to the readiness of his bride.

Since many of us live with much wreckage in our lives year after year crying out to the Lord for freedom, how do we make ourselves ready for the Lamb's wedding, for our wedding?

In fact, these answers lie in the first part of the book that is the Revelation of Jesus Christ and his bride. Note the major theme of Revelation is that of Jesus Christ. This unique revelation of him, is unveiling the pinnacle and end of history and his bride, his heart's desire.

First let us consider the problem that keeps us from being ready and the great price he paid to promise us we could be ready.

1Pet. 1:18 "knowing that you were not redeemed with perishable things like silver or gold from your futile way of life inherited from your forefathers, 19 but with precious blood, as of a lamb unblemished and spotless, the blood of Christ."

Our family of origin gave us a futile or empty way of life to a greater or lesser degree. Many families pass down much emptiness and others less. Moreover, he redeemed us from this emptiness with something far greater than silver or gold. Silver and gold are two of the world's most prized possessions. Immature believers may still strive after that which the world offers. Revelation 2-3 illustrates this for us when the glorified Bridegroom speaks to the seven churches for who he died. In this book, we will only use the Revelation 3 part.

Think of the price for a minute. He did not redeem us with the riches of man. He redeemed us by blood! Cor. 1:23 "but *we preach Christ crucified, to Jews a stumbling block and to Gentiles foolishness."* The world cannot appreciate the bridal price. If we cling to the world's lies about life and the world's systems of thought, we cannot cling to our Bridegroom and understand the price he paid for us. If you read this and believe you do not cling to the world's systems, think again. The churches of Asia, likely did not think they did either until the Lord confronted them with what he saw.

He had strong words for many in those churches and encouraging words for others. However, both groups needed to listen to his words of admonishment and caution.

Rev. 1:9 "'I, John, your brother and companion in the suffering and kingdom and patient endurance that are ours in Jesus, was on the island of Patmos because of the word of God and the testimony of Jesus.

10. "On the Lord's Day I was in the Spirit, and I heard behind me a loud voice like a trumpet,

11. "which said: 'Write on a scroll what you see and send it to the seven churches: to Ephesus, Smyrna, Pergamum, Thyatira, Sardis, Philadelphia and Laodicea."

12. 'I turned around to see the voice that was speaking to me. And when I turned I saw seven golden lampstands,

13. 'and among the lampstands was someone "like a son of man," dressed in a robe reaching down to his feet and with a golden sash around his chest.

14. 'His head and hair were white like wool, as white as snow, and his eyes were like blazing fire.

15. 'His feet were like bronze glowing in a furnace, and his voice was like the sound of rushing waters.

16. 'In his right hand he held seven stars, and out of his mouth came a sharp double-edged sword. His face was like the sun shining in all its brilliance.

17. 'When I saw him, I fell at his feet as though dead. Then he placed his right hand on me and said:"Do not be afraid. I am the First and the Last. 18. "Iam the Living One; I was dead, and behold I am alive forever and ever! And I hold the keys of death and Hades.

19. "Write, therefore, what you have seen, what is now and what will take place later.

20. "The mystery of the seven stars that you saw in my right hand and of the seven golden lampstands is this: The seven stars are the angels of the seven churches, and the seven lampstands are the seven churches."'

In the book of Revelation according to this description Jesus comes as the Judge and the conquering Lord. This Judge came to speak to the seven churches. Many believe the reference to the angel of the churches refers to the pastor of those churches. Whatever it means, the lamp stand of each church is in the hand of our Bridegroom and Judge. He judges the church before he judges the world. We will look first at the 4th church he addresses, the church of Sardis.

FOR REFLECTION

1. What futile ways of life do you practice? Ask the Lord to show you behaviors of which you are not aware. Write these in a journal and pray for his help until you are free. Freedom takes years, but he is faithful.

PRAYER

Lord help me to understand what I cannot now see. Many things influence my behavior. I cannot change what I cannot own. Help me to understand and help me to change those things that keep me from getting ready for you

CHAPTER 2
THE SARDIS PROBLEM

Rev. 3:1 "To the angel of the church in Sardis write: He who has the seven Spirits of God and the seven stars, says this: 'I know your deeds, that you have a name that you are alive, but you are dead.'"

Notice first who is speaking. It is he who holds the seven Spirits of God and the seven stars. Prior descriptions show us the one speaking is the Lord himself who was dead and is alive forever.

Rev. 1:4 "John to the seven churches that are in Asia: Grace to you and peace, from Him who is and who was and who is to come, and from the seven Spirits who are before His throne, 5 and from Jesus Christ, the faithful witness, the firstborn of the dead, and the ruler of the kings of the earth."

The seven Spirits are the Holy Spirit and we see them in the furnishings of the temple and tabernacle. (Ex 37:17) They are in heaven before his throne and in Zechariah's vision.

Zech. 4:2 'He said to me, "What do you see?" And I said, "I see, and behold, a lampstand all of gold with its bowl on the top of it, and its seven lamps on it with seven spouts belonging to each of the lamps which are on the top of it; 3 also two olive trees by it, one on the right side of the bowl and the other on its left side." 4 Then I said to the angel who was speaking with me saying, "What are these, my lord?' 5 'So the angel who was speaking with me answered and said to me, "Do you not know what these are?" And I said, "No, my lord." 6 Then he said to me, "This is the word of the LORD to Zerubbabel saying, 'Not by might nor by power, but by My Spirit,' says the LORD of hosts.'"

God gave this vision to Zerubbabel to let him know the task the Lord assigned him he would finish due to the power and might of God not by his own strength. God showed him a lamp stand with seven lights. This lamp stand is a type of the multiplicity of working of the Spirit of God. In Revelation, our Bridegroom holds this lamp stand that searches our hearts and reveals our thoughts and deeds.

The book of Revelation is the revelation of Jesus Christ. History is for his sake. He is the One who holds everything in his hand. He created not only the planet on which we live, but he created us for himself. We lose sight of this to our own peril. Unfortunately, most of the Sardis church lost sight of this truth with the result the Judge said they were dead.

The church of Sardis believed they were alive. Possibly they had rousing praise services to say nothing of marvelous liturgies. These were their actual deeds, which the Creator Lamb knows. Their deeds gave them a reputation with man, but God said they were dead. The nature of deception is that you may believe one thing about yourself, however, another thing, possibly an opposite thing is true. Hypocrisy or play-acting gave them a reputation for being alive. To those not tuned in to the Holy Spirit they may look holy. But, their deeds were not obedient to God's voice.

Churches do this today as well. They are skilled at looking alive, (" you have a name that you are alive,") but the focus is not on loving and knowing Christ and making him known to others. Jesus told the Pharisees that they made their converts twice the sons of hell as themselves *(Mt.23)*. However, the Pharisees thought they were the enlightened ones. The people followed them and held them in high honor.

Even our efforts to bring people into the "church" could bring them into a dead, play-acting church with a reputation for life, but not the life of God. Often dead religion resembles relationship with Christ due to our worship of traditions in God's place.

The standard by which we must and should measure is stated in the Ten Commandments and then restated by Christ himself.

Mark 12:29 "The most important one," *answered Jesus, "is this: 'Hear, O Israel, the Lord our* *God, the Lord is one. 30 Love the Lord your God with* *all your heart and with all your soul and with all your* *mind and with all your strength.' 31 The second is* *this: 'Love your neighbor as yourself.' There is no* *commandment greater than these."*

We can build large churches, lead great programs, do many wonderful works, but, that does not qualify us in God's eyes. Do we love him with everything within us? Do we seek him to know him or for his stuff? If we don't take time with him, do we miss him? Does our heart yearn for more time with him? Is he number one in our lives?

Spiritual death resembles the life of a star. If a star dies in the sky, it takes scores of years for that death to become obvious because of the speed at which light travels and our distance from the star.It takes time for spiritual death to become manifest to the casual observer, but the King of Kings knows the truth because he is the Righteous Judge and he sees what others cannot. The same is true of dead churches. It may be time before the death manifests to the eye of the beholder because the culture in that church accepts death as life.

God in His mercy confronts us as he did the Sardis church. He knows if the life we manifest is his life or man's idea of life. Will we listen when he sends others to tell us we have a problem?

But there was hope for Sardis. *Rev. 3:2 'Wake up, and strengthen the things that remain, which were about to die; for I have not found your deeds completed in the sight of My God."*

'The One who holds the seven stars" (the seven churches, Rev. 1:19) says, *"wake up".* This is a call to set aside apathy, self-will and self-satisfaction. There is something remaining to be strengthened in Sardis.

In the American church, we worship many mental images. Namely, the gods of comfort, convenience, mammon and individualism are major among them. Other nations worship their gods, as well. As we worship these we convince ourselves that we worship only him. Indeed, we rationalize our dedication to our mental images. They are so much a part of us they appear normal. This is hypocrisy in his eyes.

Even without our cultural idols, we bow down to mental idols from our formative years because of the futile (empty) way of life we experienced growing up in our families. Also, every country's culture and every family culture worships idols. These stand in the way of our seeing him as he is.

Hypocrisy keeps us from seeing the idols, from seeing we are dying as concerns true faith and love for the Lord. The wider culture and often the church culture keep us from seeing we are practicing dead religion instead of the life of God to which he invites us.

Yet, there was something alive in Sardis and the American church. Undeniably, there exists a faithful core, a remnant that refuses to bow the knee to the gods of this world. This remnant forsakes the family and cultural idolatry. Similarly, this remnant hears the messengers God sends. They listen to his voice in the Secret Place and search his word, see their idolatry and repent. The Glory of God addresses himself to this remnant to wake up and strengthen what remains before it too dies.

This remnant speaks forth the truth to the rest of the assembly to help waken them to love again. Often the remnant is wounded for the message, but continue on his path. This is the pattern shown in the Prophets and Psalms.

The deeds of Sardis were not complete. This could mean many things but likely it included participation in spiritual adultery, (James 4:4). It could mean they were sidetracked from God's purposes.

Rev. 3:3 'So remember what you have received and heard; and keep it, and repent.

Therefore, if you do not wake up, I will come like a thief, and you will not know at what hour I will come to you.'

Remember means to mention or discuss. A way to remember is reciting what you need to remember. Likewise, we should recount the things God has taught us. Then go back to early lessons and deeds of God and say them out loud. We must repeat the scriptural lessons he taught us in the Secret Place. These lessons set us free from the futility of our formative years. If we forget the lessons, we embrace the futility again. Deception captures our minds and keeps us from the truth and freedom we find in the Secret Place of his presence.

The Judge tells us to keep it. This means to guard it. In fact, we are to set a sentry around the things that God taught us every hour of every day. We cannot do this apart from his help. We find his help in his presence. If we are not seeking him, we will use the gifts and graces he has given to us so we can build a following, a life or a work that looks alive.

What did they receive that they should keep or guard it (obey NIV)? They were redeemed *1Pet.1:19 "with precious blood, as of a lamb unblemished and spotless, the blood of Christ."* God gave something better than gold, and the honor and acceptance that gold can buy, for each member of the bride. The bridal price paid by the Bridegroom Lamb to enter consummated relationship was his blood.

Obey is the injunction given by God to the Sardis church. Sardis was not obedient to God's voice. Further, they did not remember the great sacrifice made on their behalf. The world's promises of riches, satisfaction or honor captured them. Sardis was sleeping when they should be awake and doing His will.

The Son of God came to do the Father's will. *(Jn. 4:1, 8:28, 12:49)* He calls us to his will as well.

We speak of being transformed into his image, but what does that mean? How can we measure this? These passages give us a clue.

John 5:19 'Therefore Jesus answered and was saying to them, "Truly, truly, I say to you, the Son can do nothing of Himself, unless it is something He sees the Father doing; for whatever the Father does, these things the Son also does in like manner".

Jn. 17:4 "I glorified You on the earth, having accomplished the work which You have given Me to do."

Jn. 14:10 "Do you not believe that I am in the Father, and the Father is in Me? The words that I say to you I do not speak on My own initiative, but the Father abiding in Me does His works."

John 14: 24 "He who does not love Me does not keep My words; and the word which you hear is not Mine, but the Father's who sent Me."

John 16:13 "But when He, the Spirit of truth, comes, He will guide you into all the truth; for He will not speak on His own initiative, but whatever He hears, He will speak; and He will disclose to you what is to come."

The Father spoke to and through Jesus.

He sent the Holy Spirit to speak to and through us. Jesus did the will of the Father. Further, he spoke as the Father spoke. We can become like Jesus by beholding him. He was obedient unto death.

Beholding his death helps us carry our cross. In the meantime, we should search out his perfect obedience and perfect love as the measure of our lives. It is something we will never obtain in this life, but with our focus on him we will make progress.

He admonishes Sardis to strengthen the little that remains before it dies. If they do not wake up they miss the time of His visitation. This is a serious consequence for their lethargy. Indeed, this chastisement is one of the most serious admonitions he can give to those who claim his name. Yet, they had the Holy Spirit to help them and so do we.

Rev. 3: 4 'But you have a few people in Sardis who have not soiled their garments; and they will walk with Me in white, for they are worthy. 5 'He who overcomes will thus be clothed in white garments; and I will not erase his name from the book of life, and I will confess his name before My Father and before His angels. 6 'He who has an ear, let him hear what the Spirit says to the churches.'

Few have not soiled their clothes. This means that the rest have soiled their clothes. The few are called remnant, the over-comers within the church. These are the bride. A study of the Old Testament demonstrates that God is calling all who name him, but only a remnant of that called people will hear his call to the bride. Moreover, the remnant will walk with him dressed in white. *(For more on the remnant see Micah 4-5, Zeph. 3:13, Zech. 8:11, Rom 9:27, Rom 11:5)*

Over-comers dress in white. An over-comer is the ready bride. So, what are over-comers? It is those who commit to the process of being redeemed from the futile life handed down to them and likewise, who have allowed his grace to permeate their mess and set them free to be completely his. Further, overcomers are finding victory over the idols and lies of this life. They are not perfect, but they know God is their source. Overcomers surrender to him and make him Lord of all.

This is a notable accomplishment because the process is painful. It requires us dying to our will and becoming alive to his will. It requires*: Phil. 3:7 "But whatever was to my profit I now consider loss for the sake of Christ. 8 What is more, I consider everything a loss compared to the surpassing greatness of knowing Christ Jesus my Lord, for whose sake I have lost all things. I consider them rubbish, that I may gain Christ."*

An over-comer *"counts **everything** a loss for the sake of **knowing Christ Jesus my lord"**, Phil 3:8 (emphasis mine)*. Their treasure is not an earthly treasure. They have overcome their love of the world's offerings. In fact, their treasure is in him alone, knowing him, loving him and holding him most precious.An over-comer wears white, with unsoiled clothes and God calls them worthy. What makes them worthy of wearing white? The answer is obedience.

"Remember what you have heard: obey it, and repent." NIV.

What did they hear? He redeemed and called them to an intimate relationship. Most of the Sardis church forgot their call to be his bride. They forgot to live in close relationship with him. Sadly, this describes much of today's church. There is much activity, but little intimacy.

FOR REFLECTION

1. Are you obedient to the voice and direction of God? If not what keeps you from obedience? Confess this to him and commit to his Lordship.

2. Do you worship with people who have a reputation for being alive, but are dead? If so ask the Lord if he wants you to continue with these people. Are you a voice to them or to stay to pray for them? How can you keep intimacy alive with Jesus while there?

3. Do you remember what you have heard? Then obey it and repent and come back to the one who stands ready to receive you.

PRAYER

Terrifying Judge, Merciful Savior hear my prayer and forgive me for the futile ways I follow and the idols I serve. Set me free and make me wholly yours. I want to learn who you are. Draw me into your awesome presence so I learn to live for you and to live in your presence.

CHAPTER 3
THE CHURCH THAT IS READY

The book of Revelation is written to his bride that she might be ready. It is written so she might fulfill the deepest yearning of his ravished heart. Revelation 21 gives us a marvelous picture of his bride. Note that at the end of the book of Revelation he showcases his bride. This tells us that history so the bride becomes ready and the Bridegroom comes forth.

The letters to the churches are a specific admonition to his bride so she might be ready. When he speaks to the next church, the church of Philadelphia, he speaks of the New Jerusalem coming down out of heaven from God. *(Rev. 3:12)* This city is the bride of Revelation 21. The Bridegroom is speaking to his bride when he speaks to Philadelphia. The church or believer that has the characteristics of the Philadelphia church is the bride.

Rev. 3:7 "And to the angel of the church in Philadelphia write: He who is holy, who is true, who has the key of David, who opens and no one will shut, and who shuts and no one opens, says this:"

The name Philadelphia means brotherly love[i],[ii] Christ exhibited this when he died for us and we see this exemplified in this Philadelphia church. This means we show love one for another because of our intimate relationship with him.

The Lord's church is fragmented one from the other but the love he calls us to goes way beyond our love for our brothers in the Spirit with whom we agree. We are to love and lay our lives down for others in our world to bring them to Christ. We are to love sacrificially those who name his name even when we have differences in doctrine.

Are we willing to take up our cross daily and die to our ideas of life and become alive to his will? Will we keep our focus on him or be distracted by that which looks spiritual? Regarding this, will we buy into the world's ideas of "church"?

Years ago, many purchased jewelry that said WWJD, or (what would Jesus do). This phrase was on lanyards, purse and backpack straps, key chains and myriads of other things. It was a slogan, but few asked the question of themselves seriously. If we had asked that question, whole communities would be transformed by the love of God for the hurting, the poor and marginalized. Jesus lived a life of self-giving and obedience to the Father. If we followed him, the world could not resist His love. What **would** Jesus do?

He tells us that he has the key of David and what he opens no one can shut. *Is. 22:22* is the first time this phrase is said of Messiah. *"The key to the house of David"* is the wording in the Isaiah passage. Jesus was from David's line as regards his humanity. He is of the line of Israel's kings and is the King of Kings.

Moreover, he has authority to shut and open doors. For those who are faithful, who love him with their whole heart and do not serve other gods, he will open doors that man or evil entity cannot shut. Much of the church wants certain doors open but not other doors. The Philadelphia church is an obedient church and they wait upon the open doors he has for them. They allow his will to become their will.

He can close doors so no one can open them. This comforts those who choose his will. He can keep evil at bay and work circumstances to good. (Romans 8: 18-20.)

Rom. 8:20 "For the creation was subjected to futility, not willingly, but because of Him who subjected it, in hope 21 that the creation itself also will be set free from its slavery to corruption into the freedom of the glory of the children of God."

This passage shows He allows suffering to set us free from the futility of our upbringing and our choices. We should see this as a promise for our good, but we often run from this truth. We do this by trying to control our destiny as we evade his will for our own will. In fact, the Philadelphia Church does not fit into this mold. This church is obedient.

Rev. 3:8 'I know your deeds. Behold, I have put before you an open door which no one can shut, because you have a little power, and have kept My word, and have not denied My name.'

He knows the deeds of the Philadelphia church. Because of their deeds, he has placed before them an open door that cannot be shut. They have a little strength because they are a tiny community[iii] compared to the other churches. We see that small group again, the remnant. Though the other churches have a remnant within them this small church **is** a remnant.

They are faithful and have kept His word. Think of it this way. Revelation is written to the bride so she may know the Bridegroom's plan in the last day. He wrote it so she might understand her calling to God and ministry. She is the bride of Revelation 21. The remnant is the bride. Similarly, the Philadelphia church is the bride. The bride is in dying churches. She hears his voice. As she is amid the dying church, she rises above that death by hearing his voice. She takes a stand for his heart in that place and guards her heart from the death that surrounds her. She willingly stands alone amid the surrounding culture. Yet she is not alone for she is his.

He is her consolation when those who reject his presence reject her. She finds His presence in the Secret Place when not manifest in her church. The bride takes up her cross daily and in love and obedience carries it knowing the smile of his face is enough.

Because the bride has learned to listen to the voice of her Beloved, she sees the word of God through his heart. The word of God is her life and breath as his Spirit breathes on it. She listens for his voice continuously with the recognition that his voice alone can sustain her and change her into his image. Like the Psalmist David, she says, *"I will see Your face in righteousness; I shall be satisfied when I awake in Your likeness." Ps.17:15 NKJV.* Nothing short of this can hold her.

This bride has not denied his name. In the Old Testament times the name included character, authority and function. This was also true of the gods of the nations including the Israelite God.

Character, authority and function help the worshipper understand how to worship properly. The following passages illustrate proper worship:

Deut. 6:5 "You shall love the LORD your God with all your heart and with all your soul and with all your might." Idolatry defiles and denies His name.

Phil 2:9 "For this reason also, God highly exalted Him, and bestowed on Him the name which is above every name,

10 "so that at the name of Jesus EVERY KNEE WILL BOW, of those who are in heaven and on earth and under the earth,

11 "and that every tongue will confess that Jesus Christ is Lord, to the glory of God the Father." Phil. 2:9-11 is our heritage as His bride. We will see everyone who denied his name confess that he is Lord.

The next passage is a contrast to earlier passages. *Jer. 7:30 "For the sons of Judah have done that which is evil in My sight," declares the LORD, "they have set their detestable things in the house which is called by My name, to defile it."* Two reasons God calls this evil in his eyes is because this action denies his name and is committed in His house, in the place of his presence. In other words, adultery against him takes place in front of him. Philadelphia does not indulge in this. This church is faithful to keep her eyes on the Lord. This is not true of the whole church.

He calls us by his name. Consider Jeremiah.

Jer. 15:16 "Your words were found and I ate them, And Your words became for me a joy and the delight of my heart; For I have been called by Your name, O LORD God of hosts. "

Jeremiah's name contained part of God's name. "Ah" is a shortened form of "yah" for Yahweh. As the Lord's bride, we are called by his name. Idolatry profanes his name. Idolatry is adultery since we are his bride. But Jeremiah guarded his heart by eating, by devouring the words of God. The Lord's words were his delight.

So, what is that name we should honor and embrace?

Jer. 16:21 "Therefore behold, I am going

*to make them know — This time I will make them know My power and My might; And they shall know that My name is **the LORD**."*

*Jer. 31:35 "This is what the LORD says, he who appoints the sun to shine by day, who decrees the moon and stars to shine by night, who stirs up the sea so that its waves roar—**the LORD Almighty** is his name "*

*Jer. 32:18 "You show love to thousands but bring the punishment for the fathers' sins into the laps of their children after them. O great and powerful God, **whose name is the LORD Almighty**,"*

*Jer. 33:2 "Thus says the LORD who made the earth, the LORD who formed it to establish it, **the LORD** is His name,"*

Jer. 31:35 "Thus says the LORD, Who gives the sun for light by day, And the fixed order of the moon and the stars for light by night, Who stirs up the sea so that its waves roar; **The LORD of hosts** *is His name:"*

Jer. 33:16 "'In those days Judah will be saved and Jerusalem will dwell in safety; and this is the name by which she will be called: **the LORD is our righteousness."**

There are many scriptures that give other names for him. One truth we can gain from these scriptures is that he is Lord. Since no Lord is higher than him, we are to lay aside everything that holds our hearts to embrace him alone.

Rev. 3:9 "Behold, I will cause those of the synagogue of Satan, who say that they are Jews and are not, but lie — I will make them come and bow down at your feet, and make them know that I have loved you." The synagogue of Satan here is likely those Jews that persecuted the Christians. This occurred in Smyrna and Philadelphia at that time. [iv] As the Philadelphia church endured the persecution, the day will come when those who persecuted the church will acknowledge that the Lord loves his church. This is true of those who persecute the bride today.

Rev. 3:10 "Because you have kept the word of My perseverance, I also will keep you from the hour of testing, that hour which is about to come upon the whole world, to test those who dwell on the earth. "

Because of the Philadelphia church's faithful endurance, he would keep them from the hour of trial that will come on the entire earth. Some think this means the church will not go through the tribulation. Only God knows if this is true. One thing we understand is, the Lord keeps those who love him to the exclusion of everything else. He hides them in the Secret Place of his presence. He reserves the Secret Place for his beloved bride. The reason is that she is the only one who cares to seek him there.

Rev 3:11 'I am coming quickly; hold fast what you have, so that no one will take your crown.'

He tells those who read the book of Revelation to hold on to what you have. Do not let go no matter what others say to you. When you keep the word of the Lord and do not deny his name, crowns are stored up for you.

Two crowns are the crown of glory and the crown of life, *(James 1:12 and 1 Pet. 5:4)*. Don't let the enemy steal your crowns by deceit and the many "isms" and people he uses to spread his deceit. Further, let no one take your crown. Remember who you are and whose you are. If the bride stays connected to him, no one will take her crowns. She will have them to cast at his feet in worship for eternity.

Rev. 3:12 'He who overcomes, I will make him a pillar in the temple of My God, and he will not go out from it anymore;' This is a wonderful promise to those who yearn for him and for his presence. His beloved bride yearns for him. He is her strength, her everything while on earth, and she will live in his presence forever. There is no greater reward.

The word overcomes is the word Nikao^v in the Greek meaning to conquer. The one who conquers the idolatry and the evil presence behind it is an overcomer. Because the bride is unsure which voice is his, she runs to him. She waits until he makes himself and his truth known to her. Then the bride overcomes by his word spoken by his Spirit in his presence. She does not rely on her natural gifts of study alone. Many study without his Spirit because they study with another motive than to know him such as to impress men. Thus, they are deceived because of their wrong motive. His bride knows only his Spirit can enlighten the scriptures, so she understands what he desires. She does not study so she can have knowledge and impress men. The bride studies so she will know him and delight his heart with her love. She cries out to him and the cry of her heart is something like this:

Blazing Glory

Blazing Glory, just His blazing glory
I would see.
Just to fall at His feet as dead,
this I must be.
Dead to all, alive to Him,
dross burned out along with sin.
Blazing Glory is what I need
to destroy the weed
and the seed
of iniquity in my heart.

Blazing Glory, burning fire
purging consuming all other desires.
God formed in me, Christ within
Shining forth, convicting of sin.

Blazing Glory,
God!
I must see!!!
Deal with the sin that dwells in me!
Visit me now. Hear my heart cry!
Visit me now Lord Most High!

Blazing Glory, my only Lord
Make my heart agree with yours.
You who sit in Blazing Glory come now
this one at your feet must bow.

That Blazing Glory through me will show
and cause others to want to know.
Purify me Oh, Blazing Light,
dissipate darkness, no more night.

Blazing Glory come now come
I wait upon you my heart is numb.
But awake, alive, revived I will be,
when Blazing Glory shines through me.

Rev. 3:12b "and I will write on him the name of My God, and the name of the city of My God, the new Jerusalem, which comes down out of heaven from My God, and My new name." This is a bridal statement. Rev. 19 and 21 show us this city is the bride ready for her husband.

Consider Jeremiah. When God called him, he was young. Jeremiah did not understand the cost of the Prophet's call. Jeremiah in chapter 20 beginning in verse 1 prophesies against the temple. Because of this, a priest that is higher in rank than him has him beaten and put in the stocks. This is public humiliation for doing the will of God. He expresses his disillusionment in the next scripture.

Jer. 20:7 "O LORD, You have deceived me and I was deceived; You have overcome me and prevailed."

Jeremiah cries out to God that the Lord overcame him the same way an older man takes advantage of a younger woman. He did not expect this depth of rejection, shame and loneliness. But he bears the Lord's name. In fact, he must answer the Lord's call to prophesy the destruction of the nation he loves even though he is a tenderhearted man. His call fights against his own nature. People will reject him as he obeys and speaks.

God himself made Jeremiah a tenderhearted man yet the Lord expects and anoints Jeremiah to speak of the unimaginable destruction of the people of God. As Jeremiah obeys, he cries out.

"I never knew it could get this bad. You said you would be with me when you called me. I did not bargain for this. You withheld this information from me." It is one thing to have such a difficult message. It is another experiencing rejection by everyone because of the message. "You deceived me; you wooed me and deceived me."

God's call to Jeremiah in chapter 1 did not prepare his tender heart for the depth of rejection he was to receive. God does not reveal the whole story of our lives to us at the beginning of our calling. He tells us to count the cost. But sometimes we cannot read the small print because we are not far enough along to understand what the call and obedience to the call entails.

Over time God instructed Jeremiah not to marry or attend funerals or celebrations (Jer. 16). He was thrown in a pit, beaten and rejected by his friends. The Lord was his comfort and sometimes that was not enough. It was then he had to remember he was called by the Lord's name. He, like so many of us, faced unbearable pain and a choice. Should he walk away from the call and away from God? For the Jeremiah's of this world that is no choice. With the heart of the bride beating in his chest he must continue to follow as the cost plays out. Returning to life without God is unthinkable.

The consolation is that he does not pay that cost alone and neither do we. There is one who paid the supreme penalty and in Jeremiah's day and ours those who sought the Lord with all their hearts will find him (Jer. 29:12).

Now we understand more what this means because through Christ we see the bride revealed. Yet Jeremiah found in the Lord alone his hiding place. Jeremiah like us, was called by the Lord's name. Yah means "I Am". "I Am everything you need now or in the future." He answers every yearning in I Am if we will allow it.

One of Jeremiah's mistakes was that he assumed things when God called him. He assumed the call would be easier and more affirming than it was. He did not know the Lord as he would one day. Jeremiah needed to become an over-comer even as we do. He must overcome the persecution without blaming God for the persecution. When he blamed God, he did so because he did not yet understand the Lord's heart well.

Like Jeremiah the pain we endure is a token of what men did to the Lord, the Husband of Israel. Until we understand this, we will struggle with blaming God. We cannot understand this apart from the Lord revealing His heart to us in the Secret Place. We, like Jeremiah must overcome our expectations of how this life in God works.

Further, we must submit to God and trust his heart no matter our circumstances. Overcoming at this level is difficult work. But the Lord himself was Jeremiah's portion and consolation when he allowed him to be. The same is true of us today.

Today the following scriptures are part of our consolation along with the Lord himself.

Rev. 21:9 'Then one of the seven angels who had the seven bowls full of the seven last plagues came and spoke with me, saying, "Come here, I will show you the bride, the wife of the Lamb." 10 And he carried me away in the Spirit to a great and high mountain, and showed me the holy city, Jerusalem, coming down out of heaven from God, 11 having the glory of God. Her brilliance was like a very costly stone, as a stone of crystal-clear jasper.'"

We are being prepared as a bride for her Husband. The bride is the New Jerusalem. We will live in his presence forever.

Rev 22:4 "they will see His face, and His name will be on their foreheads.

The bride will be satisfied when she sees his face and is beholding him through eternity. He calls her by his name. He inscribes his name on her forever.

Rev. 3:13 'He who has an ear, let him hear what the Spirit says to the churches.' Are we listening? For what are we listening? Is it the world's voice, the majority's voice, the truth we want to believe or are we listening for his voice? *"He who has an ear let him hear..."* Jeremiah paid the price to hear. It was the price of rejection and the wounding of his tender heart. The least price we must pay to listen is to surrender our idols and everything dear to us. Are we listening? To the one who is listening our Bridegroom says, *"let him hear".*

FOR REFLECTION

1. Do you feel as if God deceived you? Are you struggling with bitterness against him? If you do, journal what he says to you about this problem. Give him time to give you the entire answer Sometimes we are not ready to hear what he says even though we believe we are. Other layers of deception may need removal first.

2. Are you keeping the word of the Lord? This means keeping his written word and what he has spoken to you.

3. Have you in any way denied his name? Does the way you live your life deny him?

4. What things do you need to overcome or conquer?

PRAYER

Lord, help me to keep your word and obey your voice. I live in ways that do not glorify you. Sometimes I am overcome by sin rather than overcoming sin. I want to be ready for our wedding. Show me your unbridled holiness and your unfathomable love.

CHAPTER 4
THE CHURCH THAT THINKS THEY ARE READY

Rev. 3:14 "To the angel of the church in Laodicea write:

Rev. 3:15 'I know your deeds, that you are neither cold nor hot; I wish that you were cold or hot. 16 'So because you are lukewarm, and neither hot nor cold, I will spit you out of My mouth. 17 'Because you say, "I am rich, and have become wealthy, and have need of nothing," and you do not know that you are wretched and miserable and poor and blind and naked, 18 'I advise you to buy from Me gold refined by fire so that you may become rich, and white garments so that you may clothe yourself, and that the shame of your nakedness will not be revealed; and eye salve to anoint your eyes so that you may see.'"

This letter contains a sharp admonition. The back-story to this city is that it had a textile industry that produced shiny black wool, an eye salve industry and they were rich.

Like the developed nations of our day this church lived in an area of great wealth. This wealth influenced the Laodicean church. The culture the wealth created was influencing the church rather than the church changing the culture. The result was their love for God was lukewarm like their water supply that started out cold and hot but was lukewarm when it got to their city.

God speaks to those things in which they were self-sufficient. They said they needed nothing when they were *"wretched and miserable, poor, blind and naked."* They were deceived. Though they were rich and self-sufficient according to worldly standards, they were not rich by the Lord's standards. Their pursuit of wealth kept them from seeing they were poor. They were oblivious to the truth that they were no longer seeking him with red-hot love. Their ritual of church attendance and good works was devoid of true devotion. Perhaps like much of the church in the developed nations you could "give your life to Jesus" and not be concerned with "carrying your cross".

Rev. 3: 19 'Those whom I love, I reprove and discipline; therefore, be zealous and repent.'

He was letting them know, letting today's Laodicean church know, he only comes to confront us because he loves us. In his love, he calls us to repentance. In fact, we are to repent of the belief, we can see though we are blind, we are clothed though we are naked, we are rich though we are poor.

How can his church have these problems? It is a matter of focus. Deception blinds and deceives so we cannot tell we are blind. When our focus is on the wrong things, over time we lose the ability to understand his truth. We can be rich by the world's standards, but poor by kingdom standards. If we choose our own way more than his glorious presence and way, we can easily accept a counterfeit that feels good to us. We will accept what our itching ears and wandering heart want to hear.

This means his presence may no longer be in our assemblies, but we have accepted the goose bumps of a counterfeit in place of his abiding presence. In the USA, we live in an entertainment culture and are exporting this culture across the world. Since we become like that which we behold with reverence, over time what we view often has the power to change our perspective.

Further, Westerners have felt goose bumps or tears when a movie or performance is particularly good. We do this in church as well. We judge whether we have God's presence by criteria that often has nothing to do with his presence.

This is performance-based religion's function. For example, if we believe we must perform to receive love we will seek an objective standard on which to measure our service. We find many outward measures the world, the flesh and the devil approve. Perhaps we believe we measure our fervor by dressing a certain way. It would be difficult to hear God say that was not the measure he uses.

We could believe if we dress this way we are in good standing. Trusting that what we do for works of service or obedience to the letter of the law is what he wants. We do this even though we may argue that we are justified through his blood alone and our faith in his blood alone. Our words say one thing and our lives shout another. But we cannot hear the shout of God because of deception. The problem with deception is that we do not know our deception unless we cry out for truth.

Rev. 3:20 "Behold, I stand at the door and knock; if anyone hears My voice and opens the door, I will come in to him and will dine with him, and he with Me."

He is knocking on the door of his church. What a sad commentary on the end-time church and many churches throughout the ages. When we live with abundance, we tend to shut Him out. Why not? We can do this Christian thing ourselves. Of course, we do not think this consciously. But gradually we are working our own program and he is shut out, knocking. Can you see the tears in his eyes as he knocks? He knocks and then speaks *"if anyone hears my voice, and opens the door,".* The Bridegroom Lamb is shut out knocking and asking us to open the door. Since our deception and arrogance are great in the Laodicean church, we cannot hear his plea.

He knocks on the door of congregations and the door of individuals. Many will never hear.

Rev. 3:21 "He who overcomes, I will grant to him to sit down with Me on My throne, as I also overcame and sat down with My Father on His throne."

We must overcome the enemy's deception, the futile way of life handed down from our forefathers and the idolatry that comes with that futility. Also, we must conquer the fears and arrogance that cause us to worship false gods. Another enemy of truth is the cousin to fear, the disobedience that arises out of our fear. Likewise, we must overcome our self-sufficiency and ability to work this ourselves. And most of all, we must open the door to him, so he can fellowship with us and show us our deception.

Rev. 3:22 "He who has an ear, let him hear

what the Spirit says to the churches."

Again, he asks if we can hear. Our inability to hear is a serious problem and is responsible for him being locked out of our assemblies and knocking on the door of his church. Open the door and he will come in and commune with us and us with him. Then revival will take place.

"Can you hear Me now?" He cries out. "If you can hear, listen. The Spirit is speaking."

He offers freedom from futility, freedom from the temporal and fullness of relationship with the Lamb who purchased us if we will listen and obey.

Rev. 16:15 "Behold, I am coming like a thief. Blessed is the one who stays awake and keeps his clothes, so that he will not walk about naked and men will not see his shame."

Blessed is he who buys from Him gold refined in the fire, white robes (to cover his nakedness) and eyes salve that he may see. We cannot by our cleverness or much acting produce these things. They only come from his hand. Everything we produce in our own effort is a counterfeit. Will he find us naked?

FOR REFLECTION

1. Are you worshipping the gods of the Laodicean culture around you? Name them. These gods could be arrogance, deception, money or mammon, spiritual blindness, self-righteousness, fear of exposure and others. What scriptures can take these gods captive?

2. What specific scriptures can replace your

false beliefs? Journal these then memorize the scriptures that speak the truth against the false beliefs.

PRAYER

Lord help! I am influenced by the Laodicean culture around me. I worship various idols. Help me to get free from them; all of them. Show me how to take the thoughts captive that allow these idols to reign in my life. Show me the scriptures I need to stand in to get victory over these idols.

CHAPTER 5
THE IMPOSTOR BRIDE

She doesn't mean to be an impostor. Mostly, she has no conscious thought she may be a counterfeit. Call it spiritual amnesia. There are so many spiritual forces at work, bombarding the church that all it takes is one crack, one weak block in the wall of the city through which the enemy can work. Over time, the innuendo's and deception work their intended purposes.

The chances of what seemingly began as real being replaced with the impostor bride are great because the world's systems mimic the truth. Slyly the enemy brings in the half-truths and the apathy. The half-truths sound good because we that are a part of the church have yet to allow Christ to conquer all the ground in our hearts. It is a process and takes time. Likewise, while we are growing from mental assent to yielding to total Lordship, the enemy sows his seed among the wheat and the result is catastrophic. The wheat and the tares grow together until the end. The Kingdom of Heaven is like this. (Mt. 13:24-30).

In bible times the Romans had a law against sowing tares with the wheat to sabotage an enemy for it occurred frequently. [vi] The same problem occurs in the Kingdom. There are many who believe and follow the religious system present in churches. They attend church. They even serve in gospel preaching churches. But they do not really believe. Jesus is not Lord and there is only superficial change in their lives.

Why? Scripture tells us if we believe with our heart we are saved (Rom. 10:9). The heart comprises our mind, will, and emotions. If our mind believes, but our will is not converted, if we do not embrace Lordship, then we only have a mental assent. We have not believed in our heart. Therefore, we can honor Him with our lips while our hearts are far from Him (Matt. 15:8). It is also why scripture states even the demons believe and tremble. A demon's will be not converted but they do believe.

The impostor bride and the real bride grow side by side. Tares are only evident as we move closer to the time of the harvest. The tare is the grain darnel, which means false grain. In our terms, false bride could apply. Both wheat and darnel look the same until they grow into maturity. Only then can we identify them with certainty. By then the roots intertwine and rooting up darnel could root up the wheat. So, the two must grow together until the Lord separates them at harvest time. Spiritually only he knows who the true wheat, who the true bride is. We may suspect, but it will only be revealed at harvest.

Darnel is poisonous to humans causing what resembles drunkenness. Eaten in greater quantities darnel causes convulsions[vii] and even death.[viii] Thus, we cannot eat darnel. God will destroy the darnel, the tares.

Sometimes lessons that teach us what should be, are best contrasted with what should not be, like tares among the wheat. The question in America and perhaps the world is, for who's glory do we work? Since pride is the main sign of a tare in the church, this question is important. We are called to humility and working for the King's glory. Does the Holy Spirit witness that this is true of you or your church fellowship? Listen to what you say to each other, whose glory is being brought forth? Is it God's or men's? Consider what Jesus said about this.

Luke 9:23 'Then he said to them all: 'If anyone would come after me, he must deny himself and take up his cross daily and follow me. 24 For whoever wants to save his life will lose it, but whoever loses his life for me will save it. 25 What good is it for a man to gain the whole world, and yet lose or forfeit his very self?"

We see here that just wanting to save our lives will cause us to lose them. So, only by carrying our crosses and losing our lives can we gain true life. This requires a death to self that is total. Does your life reflect this self-death or are you controlling your life and resisting the plan of God? Do you attend a church that will allow you to save your life or will they help you learn how to lose it? We sometimes choose a church fellowship that aligns with our desires for self- protection.

Perhaps you avoid close fellowship, so you do not have to suffer in relationships. Or you may ignore the call God has on your life because you do not want to appear extreme and suffer rejection by others. Likewise, you may ignore certain scriptures because to embrace them requires too much of you.

Does a job and/or church work leave little time with Him? This can help you avoid the accountability that could help you lose your life. Are you angry with God because of ways He has led you which you do not understand?

The self-death needed will be a lifetime process. Yet, we must be careful not to use that as an excuse to avoid growth. We must heed the call to come and die to self. The exciting part of this is that we become more alive unto him. In contrast, the reward of self is life that is not real. Rather, it's a counterfeit for his life.

The Revelation churches are examples of what should and should not be, both churches commended, and churches warned. What we must understand is there exists historically a counterfeit of his real, an impostor. There are those who want it easy and think God exists to serve us, make us happy, comfortable and meet our needs. In fact, whole segments of today's church teach this. This belief is big in America and we have exported it overseas.

The harlot of Revelation is a spiritual and political system characterized by idolatry. This idolatry takes many forms beyond statues of other gods. It is the worship of man's choices without God. The harlot encompasses the false religions of history including false forms of Christianity. (Rev. 17-18) So, many who were a part of the Sardis and Laodicean churches were false believers and took part in the harlot system.

We could view the attributes of these negative images and warnings from God's word and learn what we should not do. These warnings are there to help us, so we do not participate in idolatry. Read them and learn from them. They have value for searching the heart.

But, one understanding is most needful. The true bride has eyes only for her Holy Husband. She is not seeking approval, worldly riches, or the world's offerings. Her eyes focus on him and thus, her heart is his alone. She does not trade in bodies and souls of men. (Rev. 18:11-13) Rather, she loves the Lord with all her heart, soul, mind and strength and her neighbor as herself. Reaching out to others is to satisfy his heart and display his glory in the earth. Measure your own heart and the fruit of various ministries by this measure. Where do you focus your heart?

The day we are in will reveal the difference between the impostor and the true bride. In many countries where persecution is a normal part of the Christian experience, only the true bride will name his name. Pretenders are not willing to pay the price of prison, torture or death to say they belong to him. However, in countries without persecution things are not so clear. The suffering coming to any nation is a blessing to purify the church. Suffering brings forth the bride of his heart. It helps her get ready.

FOR REFLECTION

1. Are you following a system or are you following him?

2. Where do you focus your heart? If there is anything in your focus but him, repent of this and

ask his help.

3. Which of the three churches do you most resemble? Ask God to help you become the bride church of the last days.

PRAYER

Lord Help!! I cannot do this on my own. My heart wanders, but I want to focus on you alone. I know the single focus of the heart takes time. I set my heart in your direction and trust you to take me there and to bring me back to you whenever I wander. Ultimately, Lord may you be the sole focus of my life.

PART TWO-THE SOLUTIONS
CHAPTER 6
CALLED TO RADICAL OBEDIENCE AND INTIMACY

To understand intimacy with and obedience to our benevolent King, we must look to John 17. This is the prayer our Bridegroom prayed to his Father before he suffered and died.

John 17:1 "Jesus spoke these things; and lifting up His eyes to heaven, He said, 'Father, the hour has come; glorify Your Son, that the Son may glorify You, 2 even as You gave Him authority over all flesh, that to all whom You have given Him, He may give eternal life. 3 This is eternal life, that they may know You, the only true God, and Jesus Christ whom You have sent. 4 I glorified You on the earth, having accomplished the work which You have given Me to do. 5 Now, Father, glorify Me together with Yourself, with the glory which I had with You before the world was."

In this last prayer of Jesus, he speaks of the glory that comes to the Father through his death and resurrection and the eternal life that results from these events. Then he says he glorified the Father during his earthly life by obedience to accomplish the work he was given to do. The result of this was Jesus being glorified with the glory he had before he left the Father to live among us.

It would follow he calls us to the same obedience he practiced while he was with us. Further he calls us to intimacy. He expects us to have conversations with him as a bride has with her husband. Jesus practiced this intimacy with the Father when he walked among us. Though these two things may seem opposite in American culture or any democracy, they are not in the Kingdom of Heaven.

He is a King. He is the King of all other Kings and therefore, deserves and must have total obedience. Our King presides over a kingdom not a democracy. Because he is all-knowing he knows best. The Lord does not demand obedience because he is a megalomaniac, He knows best because he is God.

He is also love. Jesus is the One who created everything we can see so he could have a bride with which to fellowship and to whom He could show his great love. If we stay connected to him intimately, we will discover that obedience brings with it more intimacy. We will understand we can trust his heart and his love and he will only do us ultimate good.

Most of us agree with the above statements if we have attended a gospel preaching church. But many of us do not actually practice obedience and trust and, thus, we have little intimacy with him.

Is. 50:10-11 teaches us an important lesson:

10 "Who is among you that fears the LORD, That obeys the voice of his servant, That walks in darkness and has no light? Let him trust in the name of the LORD and rely on his God.

11 "Behold, all you who kindle a fire, Who encircle yourselves with firebrands, Walk in the light of your fire And among the brands you have set ablaze. This you will have from My hand:

You will lie down in torment."

The first point of this passage is the person who fears the Lord obeys. Then scripture tells us how obedience looks. If we walk in darkness, we are to trust in the name of the Lord and rely on him.

The name of the King described who he was. The banners the troops carried into battle have the name of the King emblazoned on them. If the king's name was great, other nations that were inferior seeing this would tremble in fear.

There is no higher name than our God. No power can stand against him. So, we can trust him in every circumstance. But we struggle with this until we learn better.

Verse 11 tells us what we must not do. When darkness is all we can see, we are not to light our own light or we will lie down in torment. When we do not trust God, we are moving in fear and *"fear has torment"* 1 Jn. 4:18. In fact, the word torment is better translated as punishment and is present tense. So, punishment is now, ongoing and inherent in the fear. If we indulge fear the punishment continues.

It is best said fear is the punishment. Because we fear and do not trust we light our own fires until we learn that does not work. Lighting our own fire is an attempt to ease our suffering due to, the event that brought the darkness. What happens instead is more suffering either as ongoing or deeper suffering due to the fear to which we yielded. The fear is the cause of the suffering.

So often we think of obedience as something that God wants us to do or a great call of God we need to fulfill. Often obedience is staying in the dark until he brings the light or remaining faithful in winter until he brings the spring. This requires trusting with all our heart. (Prov. 3:5-6) Trust is a process and develops over time as we wait on God. Our part is to choose trust while waiting in the darkness.

A friend told me a true story. On his way to a commuter train he saw a woman with a sign that said, "Obey God". It was frigid and snowing. So, he approached her and asked, "Ma'am, why are you holding that sign out here in this weather?" She told him, "Because I did not obey God."

He got on his commuter train and was sitting there mulling over this conversation when God said to him, "Pray with these people." He jumped up and said to the people present, "Could you bow your heads while we pray." Then he prayed for those present as they bowed their heads.

The woman's experience put the fear of God in him. Can you imagine the commuter's conversation around their dinner tables that night?

Obedience and trust are keys to intimacy. Jesus partook of our human condition, so he might understand what we face and be made perfect through suffering *(Heb. 2).* This is the reason he is qualified to judge us. He partook of our humanity, so he could understand first-hand the things that tempt us. Then he tells us in *Heb. 3:1 NIV* that because of what he did, we are to fix our thoughts on Jesus. Fixing our thoughts is a key to obedience and trust. The thought patterns we are used to would keep us looking to our own devices. When we do not trust, we spend our time trying to make life work.

Hebrews gives us more insight. *Heb. 3:7 " Therefore, just as the Holy Spirit says, 'Today if you hear His voice, 8. Do not harden your hearts as when they provoked Me, As in the day of trial in the wilderness,'"*

First, we must understand that today is the day we hear his voice. We often live in the past with regrets and a sense of failure. We also live in fear of the future. These things keep us from hearing his voice today. We must make a conscious choice to hear his voice. If we do not, like the Israelites in the wilderness, we harden our hearts. The more we choose disobedience and lack of trust because of wounds of the past and fear of the future the harder our hearts become.

Matt. 7:21 "Not everyone who says to Me, 'Lord, Lord,' will enter the kingdom of heaven, but he who does the will of My Father who is in heaven will enter. 22 Many will say to Me on that day, 'Lord, Lord, did we not prophesy in Your name, and in Your name cast out demons, and in Your name perform many miracles?' 23 "And then I will declare to them, 'I never knew you; depart from Me, you who practice lawlessness.'"

This scripture is clear. There are some who believe they are serving God, but if they work their own agenda, even if they seem to move in the spiritual gifts listed throughout the New Testament, they practice lawlessness.

In fact, the word rendered provoked in *Heb. 3:8* in the New American Standard Version the NIV interprets as rebellion. When we refuse to obey and refuse to listen, so we might know what to obey, we are practicing rebellion and lawlessness.

The root of rebellion, disobedience and lawlessness is fear. We rebel and disobey because we do not trust God's heart for us. Fear that his will is not our best option stalks us. We fear because we do not know him. If we knew him, we would understand that we can trust him to always work for our ultimate good. (For more about fear read *Bridegroom's Song*.)

This next scripture shows what it looks like when one is truly converted.

1John 2:15 "Do not love the world or anything in the world. If anyone loves the world, the love of the Father is not in him. 16 For everything in the world — the cravings of sinful man, the lust of his eyes and the boasting of what he has and does — comes not from the Father but from the world. 17 The world and its desires pass away, but the man who does the will of God lives forever."

The person who does God's will inherits eternal life. How can this be? We could believe with our mind and change many behaviors even entering full time Christian work yet are not converted. Our will must undergo conversion. When our will is converted, our emotions will follow. If due to fear of the future, our emotional wounds and self-interest we do not choose to obey, we may not be truly His. If we choose the world's ways, rather than obedience scripture tells us the love of the Father is not in us.

Babies are not good at obeying until trained by their parents. Even Jesus learned obedience through suffering. So, these scriptures are not referring to believers early in the process of growth. These scriptures refer to yielding to his Lordship over the whole of our life. New believers must yield their will many times until yielding becomes a way of life.

Rom. 6:11 "In the same way, count yourselves dead to sin but alive to God in Christ Jesus. 12 Therefore do not let sin reign in your mortal body so that you obey its evil desires."

If we do not obey God and choose the truth that we are dead to sin, we will instead obey sin. One reason for this response is found in *John 10:10 "The thief comes only to steal and kill and destroy; I have come that they may have life and have it to the full."* The word steal means to steal by deception. Deception rules our lives before knowing Christ and after coming to him we still struggle in many areas. The enemy first deceives then he kills and destroys.

Because of this, he tells us to fix our thoughts on Jesus and consider his suffering. This helps us understand that he only wants our good. If we consider what he said and did, we learn that he is trustworthy. But, if we choose to live by the lies we believe about life, we will not make the correct choices. Notice the word choice and choices throughout this chapter. This is no accident; obedience and trust are always a choice.

Prov. 3:5 "Trust in the Lord with all your heart and lean not on your own understanding; 6 in all your ways acknowledge him, and he will make your paths straight."

The instruction to trust is a command. Again, we can opt to trust or not. He instructs us to trust with all our heart and scripture tells us how to do this. We are to lean not on our own understanding. To trust we must make a conscious choice to lean on God. This means giving up our will and agenda and choosing to believe God's plan for us is best. We cannot do this without the Holy Spirit's help. But God lives within us to help us live the life to which He calls us.

So, *Hebrews 3:1* tells us to fix our thoughts on Jesus or consider and understand him. And *Hebrews 12:2-3* tells us to fix our eyes on him.

Heb. 12:2 "Let us fix our eyes on Jesus, the author and perfecter of our faith, who for the joy set before him endured the cross, scorning its shame, and sat down at the right hand of the throne of God. 3 Consider him who endured such opposition from sinful men, so that you will not grow weary and lose heart."

Again, we must choose to fix our eyes on Jesus. In fact, we must choose him moment-by-moment and hour-by-hour. He will perfect our faith, but he cannot if we do not choose Him. *"for the joy set before Him He endured the cross."*

We were the joy "set before Him" and he showed us how to choose obedience, trust and intimacy. If we set him before us, if we see him and fix our thoughts on him, we will become like him. When he died, he showed us how to live, how to die and how to fix our focus on him. The book of Hebrews talks of a Sabbath rest into which we are to enter. This rest is impossible apart from obedience. The concept of Sabbath rest means we cease from our own works. What this means is we work the works of God. We obey. To obey we must trust. *Hebrews 3:18-19* tells us the Israelites could not enter the rest of God in the wilderness due to disobedience. Verse 19 says they did not enter because of unbelief. Unbelief precedes disobedience.

We must choose trust and obedience despite evidence to the contrary. But we struggle. So, God gave us instruction to help us.

Heb. 4:12 "For the word of God is living and active. Sharper than any double-edged sword, it penetrates even to dividing soul and spirit, joints and marrow; it judges the thoughts and attitudes of the heart. 13 Nothing in all creation is hidden from God's sight. Everything is uncovered and laid bare before the eyes of him to whom we must give account."

Heb. 4:14 "Therefore, since we have a great high priest who has gone through the heavens, Jesus the Son of God, let us hold firmly to the faith we profess 15 For we do not have a high priest who is unable to sympathize with our weaknesses, but we have one who has been tempted in every way, just as we are — yet was without sin. 16 Let us then approach the throne of grace with confidence, so that we may receive mercy and find grace to help us in our time of need."

Along with fixing out thoughts and eyes on Jesus, we need to apply the living and active word of God to our lives. For this reason, we must read and study the word. We must speak the truth against the deception that we are told about in *John 10:10*. First the enemy steals by deception, then he kills the life and truth of God and then he destroys the lives of men. But the word of God penetrates and divides everything and shows what really exists. Therefore, we must be warriors in the word and hold firmly to the faith. We have mercy and the grace of God to help us if we will receive his provision in faith.

We must stand against the lies of the enemy and not continue to give territory to him in our lives. Our choice must be for the Bridegroom no matter how difficult the path. He chose us.

We possess the living and active word, and the presence of our Holy God living in our lives to help us choose truth, obedience and intimacy with him.

FOR REFLECTION

1. If you have an area where you are struggling with trust? Confess this to the Lord. Then listen to hear what he says. Keep this problem before him in prayer until you resolve it.

2. Listen to the Lord for any areas of disobedience in your life. Confess your sin as he shows you. Listen for what he says to you about it. Continue to hold this before him in prayer until resolved.

PRAYER

Lord help me to quit lighting my own fire but wait upon you in the darkness. Empower me to trust with my whole heart, trust your word and apply it to my life. I fix my eyes upon you. Help me to continue to do so.

CHAPTER 7
INTIMACY REQUIRES HEARING

Obedience requires hearing the voice of God and hearing intimately connects us to God. We cannot obey if we cannot hear and we cannot hear if we do not take time to listen. If we marry someone and then never listen to the heart of our spouse, we will not have a successful marriage.

Song of Songs 1:2 "May he kiss me with the kisses of his mouth! For your love is better than wine."

Do you remember when you first came to know him, and you were in his word and worshipped and adored him constantly? The word wine in this passage is a symbol of blessing. His presence was better than any blessing. This can wane over time. Often it happens due to familiarity or busyness. Has he become so familiar or you are so busy that you no longer desire him as you once did? Perhaps, you are not seeking intimacy with him but have moved from relationship to religious duty.

Song 1:4 gives us another look at the first blush of knowing Him.

"Take me away with you—let us hurry! Let the king bring me into his chambers."

In this passage the word chambers means his innermost apartment. The bride is crying out for him to draw her into intimacy with him. In the timeline of the Song she has just met him. She has yet to experience the betrothal and the consummation of the marriage. But she is thinking ahead wanting to experience the closeness that comes because of marriage. This yearning is a part of the new believer's experience. It is meant to be a part of our lives over the years as the next passage of scripture shows us.

Ps. 27:4 "One thing I have asked from the Lord, that I shall seek: That I may dwell in the house of the Lord all the days of my life, "To behold the beauty of the Lord, and to meditate in His temple. "

Notice this says all the days of my life. It also highlights meditating in His temple. This includes hearing his voice.

Revelation 21 shows us his city with the Lamb as our lamp. Forever we will behold his beauty and meditate on his glory, grace, love and his other attributes. Further, we are to desire this now.

His heart desiring fellowship with us is displayed in the following:

Song 2:10

"My beloved responded and said to me, 'Arise, my darling, my beautiful one, And come along. 11 'For behold, the winter is past, The rain is over and gone. 12 'The flowers have already appeared in the land; The time has arrived for pruning the vines, And the voice of the turtledove has been heard in our land. 13 'The fig tree has ripened its figs, And the vines in blossom have given forth their fragrance. Arise, my darling, my beautiful one, And come along!'"

God speaks this to the bride after she has endured a long winter season. Winter was so long in fact, she finds herself reluctant to respond. Winter caused her to question all she guided her life by and it wounded her so deeply that hope is missing from her life.

Without winter, spring has no meaning and no extra joy. It is because of the promise of spring after the confinement and dreariness of winter we find ourselves with renewed hope. That which seems dead sprouts with life we had forgotten was possible. This discourse above by the Bridegroom is the first hint that spring and hope may be possible

Winter Season
Winter, dead, barren, cold,
stretching on it seems forever.
No fruitfulness, no life, nothing to give hope.
Joy lies frozen under the snow.
It seems that never again will life flourish.
All is gone.

But then the crocus blooms
through the cold.
That which seemed forever was transient.
The barrenness ends with the melting.
And joy blooms again.

Many have experienced winter that is so deep the concept of spring has become foreign. Due to years of winter without spring, it becomes impossible to think of change. It is in this dark season that the Lord comes to us to say spring is here. We have a choice. We can stay where we are, so we do not risk more pain, or we can trust him and go with him. But, he does not tell us where he is taking us only that he invites to come with him. He yearns to journey with us. Then he invites us into his presence.

Song 2:14

> *"O my dove, in the clefts of the rock,*
> *In the secret place of the steep pathway,*
> *Let me see your form,*
> *Let me hear your voice;*
> *For your voice is sweet,*
> *And your form is lovely."*

He invites us into the secret place of his presence. It is along a steep pathway, but we have known little else. Rather, the mountains of difficulty have been our life. Will we climb again?

That which helps us choose him is the rest of his words to us. He wants to see our form and hear our voice. Our voice is sweet, and we are lovely to him. During long years of winter with no spring one thing remains true for his bride. She loves him and longs to be with him. In fact, no matter how deep the pain and how unhealed the wounds which he allowed, she wants him.

If you are being invited out of that winter season hear his invitation. *"Let me see you, let me hear your voice, for you voice is sweet, and you are lovely."* Winter has told you otherwise, but his invitation is the truth. Will you choose the truth he speaks to you or the lie of winter?

Song 4:8 "Come with me from Lebanon, my bride, 9"You have stolen my heart, my sister, my bride; you have stolen my heart with one glance of your eyes, with one jewel of your necklace."

Again, and again throughout Song of Songs He cries out with yearning for us. He invites us to travel with him. He describes the way he sees us.

There are four in-depth descriptions of us in Song of Songs. (For more on this subject read *Bridegroom's Song*.) These descriptions show us what he saw when he went to Calvary for us. *"who for the joy set before him endured the cross, scorning its shame" (Heb. 12:2).* We were the joy set before him. Song of Songs describes what he saw as he walked the way to Calvary and death. He fixed his eyes on us, so he could die for us.

He created the world, so he could have a bride, so he could have you. This God of all gods yearns for fellowship with you. This King, this God of all Gods wants you. He yearns for you now and wants you to be ready to spend eternity with him in fellowship so sweet, no language can fully describe it.

The book of Genesis begins with intimacy with man in the garden. The book of Revelation ends with intimacy with the bride as the New Jerusalem. **History is the story of his desire for intimacy with us.**

Gen. 3:8 "And they heard the voice of the Lord God walking in the garden in the cool of the day:" The Lord communed with Adam and Eve by His voice. In the garden, they had what we long for, God speaking to them regularly. Man, lost this through sin but in Christ's death restored it, if we will have it.

In *Ex. 19* He told the Israelites if they obeyed his voice he would make them his own possession or treasure, a kingdom of priests and a holy nation. But they did not consent to be led by his voice *(Ex.*

19 and Jere. 7:22-25). Being led by his voice means intimacy and requires obedience.

Obedience without intimacy is law. Intimacy is not possible without obedience for disobedience breaks the covenant and stops the voice of God.

So, Christ died to establish the covenant by his voice with all who respond to the invitation to intimacy and obedience.

Then in *Revelation 21* we see the bride as a city with the Lord himself the light of that place. His glory is the illumination of the bride. Her heart has sought the light of that glory, the light of that blessed face for the whole of her Christian experience. She came to understand while here on earth that obedience's great reward is intimacy with Christ. There exists no better reward in this life or the next, and no price of obedience too high to eclipse intimacy's glory.

Do not allow the enemy's strategies to steal this great love. There is none greater, and it is meant for you. It requires trust, so you can choose obedience.

Trust requires the word of God to be woven into the tapestry of our lives replacing the threads of lies woven by the enemy. Believers must be violent about this. We must seize his truth as if only this can save our lives because only his truth can.

Choosing this love and our Lover again and again over every surrounding enticement must become our life. We must give up control and surrender as a bride to her bridegroom on her wedding night. All she knows is that the one who paid her bridal price with his blood loves her.

FOR REFLECTION

1. Confess to the Lord your wrong attitudes toward intimacy. Tell him what you will change.

2. What have you discovered in this chapter that helps you understand his red-hot love. Journal this and read it over these next few weeks until your ideas about his love change permanently.

PRAYER

The longer I know you Lord the more I realize that I cannot think correctly unless you redeem every thought and motivation of my heart. Help me will to do your will. Help me to desire you above all else and to stop my wrongheaded ways of thinking. I want to seek you more than the air I breathe. Be merciful and take me there. Only you can change me. I yield to you my Husband, my Bridegroom, my King.

CHAPTER 8

PUT ON YOUR WEDDING GARMENT

Scripture tells us we are to put on Jesus Christ, put on our wedding garment, and put on faith and love (1Thess. 5:8), plus our new self (Eph. 4:20-28) and our armor (Eph. 6). Further, we must put off our old self. As his bride, we must understand what we should put off and what we should put on. Ultimately, we are to put on a bridal garment. But, what is this bridal garment and how do we get it? For a general understanding of wedding garments this parable of Jesus gives us a first look:

Matt. 22:1 "'Jesus spoke to them again in parables, saying, 2 "The kingdom of heaven may be compared to a king who gave a wedding feast for his son. 3 "And he sent out his slaves to call those who had been invited to the wedding feast, and they were unwilling to come. 4 "Again he sent out other slaves saying, 'Tell those who have been invited, "Behold, I have prepared my dinner; my oxen and my fattened livestock are all butchered and everything is ready; come to the wedding feast."' 5 "But they paid no attention and went their way, one to his own farm, another to his business, 6 and the rest seized his slaves and mistreated them and killed them.'"

This passage states that the King invited people to a wedding feast, but they chose not to come. In addition, this passage shows us four ways we may refuse to get ready for the wedding feast.

To get ready they would have to put off their plans and accept the King's plan or in other words, exchange their will and plans for his will and plans. So, one lesson in this scripture is a willingness to do the King's will.

These unwilling to attend could be the unsaved who hear the message and decide against it. These can also be those who agree intellectually with the message that Jesus is Savior and Lord, but do not embrace Lordship and heart belief.

In today's church, many believe this way. Further, we have so watered the gospel we tell people if they believe Jesus is Savior he will make life easier. We don't tell them it will cost them everything and they will need to make him Lord of All. Many today attend our churches and think they are "saved", but there is no life change because there was no true conversion.

There are many cultural Christians. They have grown up in the church and know doctrine. These worship, sing in choir, attend bible study but they do not know him as Lord and Savior. They embrace Christian culture, but they have not embraced him.

The second group in this parable paid no attention because they were too busy making a living or serving. One went off to his field another to his business. This could mean busy with church work. When "church" becomes the focus rather than intimately knowing the Lord, we can miss his invitation all the while thinking we are serving him. We can tell ourselves we are serving him while we are serving our egos or our scarred sense of self.

When self is deeply wounded, we can develop behaviors of service to others that help us feel better but keep us from the Lord himself. These behaviors can find their expression in Christian service.

Sometimes Christian service is done to receive praise from others and hold a feeling of worthlessness at bay. Others want the praise of men because they believe they deserve it. In addition, many in this category quote scriptures about salvation being only by grace, but they serve to win points with God or people. Others may serve to prove to themselves they are performing well enough to be loved and accepted.

Those who paid no attention were saying the wedding banquet is not important enough to even notice. The King's heart desire was not their focus. Instead, one went to his farm another to his business. They were busy with other things because they do not know the King's heart.

Mark 4:18 "And others are the ones on whom seed was sown among the thorns; these are the ones who have heard the word, 19 but the worries of the world, and the deceitfulness of riches, and the desires for other things enter in and choke the word, and it becomes unfruitful."

This group has unfruitful soil. They have not allowed the Lord to help remove the thorns in their soil. They hang on to that which makes them idolaters. Many say they worship god, but they really worship their accomplishments. They get their sense of worth from their performance rather than from the One who gave himself for them. Not only are their riches deceitful, so is their heart. They have not made Jesus Lord and his cross central. Further, they did not allow him to transplant his heart within them in exchange for their heart of stone. Indeed, humans hang on to and called truth. They involve themselves in the world system characterized by the harlot but are unaware. The watered-down understanding of the role of the cross in today's church culture keeps them from seeing the truth.. Unlike the bride who learned to forsake the world, those who pay no attention to the King, seek the world and its enticements and continue to do so.

Many true believers likely did the same for a season and then have seen their performance-based orientation and their idolatrous life style and repented. In fact, they put off the world's ways and submitted to God, putting on Christ. Their soil is free of thorns

The next type of person who did not go to the wedding banquet persecuted those who carried the message. In the end, they killed the King's servants. Likely, they did this because they did not agree with the message, or felt it was "too much". That could mean too much commitment or time, too much to ask, too much of their divided heart expected. They did not want to hear the message to attend the wedding banquet because it required something from them.

This message is what Jesus came to Earth to deliver. He is the Bridegroom. The bridal price was his life. Most of the religious leaders of the day missed him. For the Pharisees, his claims to be God, his cry against their hypocrisy and religious duplicity were "too much". The Pharisees blamed and shamed him, put him on public display then killed him. What is more, they said it was his fault. The same happens to many servants of the King today.

Another cause of persecution is envy. Scripture tells us Jesus died because the Pharisees envied him. He was a threat to their power over the people. *(Mk. 15:10, Ja.3: 14-16)*.

Those who do not affirm the call to the wedding banquet for the Son may, like the Pharisees persecute those who call them to the banquet. This has been happening throughout the ages. Likewise, it happens today. Persecution comes to those who call out to invite the church to know him as Bridegroom. The attitude of the Pharisees that caused the death of the Bridegroom is still active. Those persecuted today are told it happens because it's their fault, they are the problem and their message is "too much".

Those who persecuted the messengers the King sent believed the message to come to the wedding banquet was antithetical to their truth or that their truth was more important. Indeed, many do not believe getting ready for the wedding banquet is important if we get our doctrine "right". Right doctrine is an important step in the Christian life, but we can twist doctrine and make it into error. In like manner, we can call our own ideas doctrine and teach them to others. This then is knowledge but not truth. Doctrine is one facet of a beautiful precious stone. Intimate relationship is another facet. Sadly, if we have knowledge without relationship, we can become prideful about our knowledge and stuck there.

In relationship, we hear his voice and he reveals the scriptures to us. His Spirit helps us understand what the word means. To put it another way if we try to understand without the Spirit we end up with church splits and denominations. Church history is littered with attempts to determine belief apart from the Spirit of God. The scripture below shows the underlying attitude of the "church" of Jesus' day.

Mark 7:6 "Rightly did Isaiah prophesy of you hypocrites, as it is written:

'THIS PEOPLE HONORS ME WITH THEIR LIPS, BUT THEIR HEART IS FAR AWAY FROM ME. 7 'BUT IN VAIN DO THEY WORSHIP ME, TEACHING AS DOCTRINES THE PRECEPTS OF MEN.' 8 "Neglecting the commandment of God, you hold to the tradition of men."

The Pharisees convinced themselves that their doctrine was correct, but they missed the Bridegroom. They worshipped in vain. They studied much, but they did not study to know God. Instead, they studied to impress men (*Matt. 23).*

Man's doctrines can lead us to kill the messengers the King sends to us to invite us to the wedding banquet. The Pharisees did this when the Bridegroom himself invited them. On the other hand, if we don't kill them we can reject them, exclude them, shame them and tell them the persecution is their fault.

It is important that we allow the Lord to cleanse our hearts of our improper motives, so we can get ready for the wedding, so we can put on our wedding garment. Notably, the most important thing we can do is get ready. For this we need to look past earth's rewards and keep our focus on the Lord, our heavenly reward.

FOR REFLECTION

1. Ask the Lord to show you if you are refusing the message to get ready for the wedding. Write whatever he shows you and pray until he tells you your heart is in alignment with his.
2. Are you a cultural Christian or is Jesus Lord of All? Do you live for your own plans or for him? Commit to him today to make him Lord of every aspect of your life.
3. If you harmed his messengers talk to God about this and make it right with him and with those you harmed.
4. Are there messengers you thought were too much? Ask the Lord to show you if they brought his message. He often sends people in the 'John the Baptist' mode to speak to his people. What message did they come to bring? Ask the Lord to help you understand their message.

PRAYER

Bridegroom Lamb grant me forgiveness for treating the desire of your heart so lightly. I could not see the truth. Draw me ever nearer so I can respond with total love to You.

Empower me to be willing to be made ready. Draw me Lord. Help me be willing to say yes to each step you call me to on this journey. I give you permission to drag me there if you must. Do not leave me in my present condition but draw me on into the center of your will. May your will become more important to me than my next breath.

CHAPTER 9
PUTTING OFF THE OLD AND PUTTING ON THE NEW

There is a fourth way the King's subjects refused the King.

Matt. 22:11 "But when the king came in to look over the dinner guests, he saw a man there who was not dressed in wedding clothes, 12 "and he said to him, 'Friend, how did you come in here without wedding clothes?' And the man was speechless. 13 "Then the king said to the servants, 'Bind him hand and foot, and throw him into the outer darkness; in that place there will be weeping and gnashing of teeth.' 14 "For many are called, but few are chosen."'

The King invited these guests to the wedding banquet after the first group refused. The custom was for the King to give wedding clothes to wedding guests sponsored by him in that day. This is also true of the bride according to *Revelation 19:7-8*. However, the man in this story chose not to wear the clothes the King provided. He thought the clothes he owned were good enough. So, what does the King expect of us?

This parable sets between two diatribes by Jesus against the Pharisees. So, we could assume that the Lord 's message in these other two parables is related to the answer. He addresses the Pharisees hypocrisy in the two parables that bookend this passage. Hypocrisy is the Greek word for an actor. Hypocrisy, play-acting and our own rationalization and denial keep us from seeing the lies within our lives. Unbelievably, we choose hypocrisy even if not consciously. We do this to stop future hurt. We devise a false identity we believe will keep people from knowing the "truth", the horrible shame that got us hurt.

This false identity covers up the "real" identity we have. Real is in quotes because the real identity is not real either, but we believe it of ourselves and we are shamed by it. Others put this identity on us by their actions or the enemy's tactics and lies. Sadly, even though it's a lie, it has become ours and we own it and protect it as if it were precious.

This happens while we are young. Because we are young, we think no one must know, so we devise this more pleasing identity. We put on a mask announcing this new identity to anyone we meet. No one can know the "truth" about us. Isaiah spoke of this problem thousands of years ago.

IS. 28:15C "For we have made falsehood our refuge and we have concealed ourselves with deception."

Or to say it another way we made lies our refuge and have hidden ourselves with those lies. The Lord must become our refuge not the lies we accept about ourselves.

At odds with these two false identities is our real identity as believers. We are in Christ. We are his, chosen, set apart and dearly loved. But, often we only pay these truths lip service because we are so busy playing the role that goes with our mask or masks. Instead, we are busy covering up what we perceive as the "real" us, but it's not real at all. It is a lie perpetrated by the enemy and meant to shame us, bind us and drive us to hypocrisy. The enemy loves hypocrisy. He loves acting. He acts because he lies all the time.

We present this self to others instead of embracing the truth. The work of God is to set us free from the false identity that deceives us and keeps us from him. This takes years and much time in his word and presence. We cannot put on our wedding garment when this clothes us first. We believe we are clothed and need nothing *(Rev. 3:17)*. So, we refuse the wedding garment.

In brief, in the Greek theatre of bible times the hypocrite (actor) has several masks in their hand. They put up a different mask for each part they played. Undeniably, this presents a picture of what we do to survive emotionally when we experience brokenness inside and are not yet healed.

The man without wedding clothes was saying, "What I am wearing (which announces who I believe I am) is good enough". "I don't need what the King gives." These are the sins of pride and self-sufficiency. They are two things that commonly go with false identities. He was saying, "I am rich and need nothing." *(Rev. 3:17)* He needed to put off what he was wearing to put on what the King provided.

This man made a conscious choice to not wear what the King provided. We do too unless we submit to the process that sets us free. We do not realize we are wearing a deceptive identity. What we believe about ourselves must be put off to receive the truth. Our deception is so deep, we cannot see the truth unless we decide to live a life of total commitment. Only as we commit and recommit to knowing God will he be able to bring freedom to us. Indeed, in his presence and through suffering he can show us our false self (idol). Because suffering is a part of this process, a belief system without carrying our cross daily can keep us from the healing we need.

Have you even known someone amid a conflict with other friends or family? They keep on telling you who they are and stating, "I am not that kind of person." But, you notice they are the instigator or at least part of the problem. You have just seen the action of a false identity. The scripture states that the heart of man is wicked and beyond our knowing *(Jer. 17:6)*. We often think we know ourselves when we do not. This is because deception blinds us to the truth. The Lord knows our hearts, however (Rev. 2:23).

This false identity does not always announce itself well. Since false identities hide under protective layers, we have trouble seeing through them. We can portray what we believe in very subtle ways. We rarely know why we do the things we do.

Rom. 13:11 "Do this, knowing the time, that it is already the hour for you to awaken from sleep; for now, salvation is nearer to us than when we believed. 12 "The night is almost gone, and the day is near. Therefore, let us lay aside the deeds of darkness and put on the armor of light. 13" Let us behave properly as in the day, not in carousing and drunkenness, not in sexual promiscuity and sensuality, not in strife and jealousy. 14 "But put on the Lord Jesus Christ and make no provision for the flesh in regard to its lusts."

In the passage above there is an urgency to awaken from sleep and get dressed. We are to put on armor and the Lord Jesus Christ. Before either of these can take place however, we must lay aside the deeds of darkness. To put on the day's clothing, we must take off whatever we wore to sleep. Also, armor must be worn over something or it rubs our skin raw. So, we put off darkness and put on Christ and his righteousness.

Laying aside the deeds of darkness includes not carousing. Carousing was often a loud party that paraded through the streets giving honor to another god with sexual debauchery.[ix]

Sex was worship to these other gods. It still is today. We worship our gods of sexual license in many nations.

We are to put off drunkenness, sexual promiscuity, sensuality, strife and jealousy. These things can keep us from putting on our armor, our wedding garment and the Lord Jesus Christ.

Think of this. Carousing included honor to other gods. In fact, these gods were so much a part of the culture they did not recognize them as wrong. Idolatry could be the reason the King's subjects were not ready. Service to many gods may distract you too much to see the urgency to get ready. In prosperous nations, some of those gods are, comfort, convenience, mammon, leisure, entertainment, selfishness, etc.

In *Matthew 22* the gods served could have been the gods who promised abundant crops or business success. Certainly, those who did not come to the banquet felt that serving their own agenda, their idol god, was more important than serving the king. The *Matthew 22* passage starts with the statement *"the kingdom of heaven is like"*. Thus, the Lord was saying this is what those who claim to be his church do in practice.

In *Rom. 13* the root words that make up the word strife literally mean to have "conquest over a friend"-x. Often, we do not recognize this as keeping us from putting on our armor, our wedding garment and the Lord Himself. Instead, we believe we are justified in our disputes. When you see strife and jealousy together it makes sense to look at the book of James to uncover what the Lord is saying.

James 3:13 "Who among you is wise and understanding? Let him show by his good behavior his deeds in the gentleness of wisdom. 14 But if you have bitter jealousy and selfish ambition in your heart, do not be arrogant and so lie against the truth. 15 This wisdom is not that which comes down from above, but is earthly, natural, demonic. 16 For where jealousy and selfish ambition exist, there is disorder and every evil thing".

NIV renders the words bitter jealousy as bitter envy. The reason is that the word bitter is used to describe this emotion. Envy and jealousy have different meanings. Envy is jealousy together with bitterness and selfish ambition. Though envy and jealousy have a shared meaning in wanting something someone else has, envy takes it several steps further. The one who envies must dispossess the person envied. Even if the envious cannot have what the envied person has, they must wrestle the coveted object from the one envied. Often this object is the person's good standing in a congregation or group.

They want to control the person and thereby control their gifts. An example is Jezebel. She dispossessed Naboth of his vineyard by having him killed. Indeed, she dispossessed the true prophets of their position by killing them. She controlled the Baal prophets (they ate at her table) thereby controlling the prophetic. Today the envious still work to control God's voice to his people.

Selfish ambition, is a perverted form of self-love and causes this. A synonym for selfish ambition is strife. Some translations translate the words selfish ambition as strife. Wherever this arises there is strife and every evil work.

The envious are *"arrogant and lie against the truth"*. Why would they do this? They cannot admit the problem is in their heart and choose blindness to their sin. They choose their sin rather than to put on the Lord Jesus Christ. If they were to see their problem, their idol, they would have to suffer to see it. That is true of all our false beliefs.

Suffering is the road to freedom. Those who envy cause others to suffer and insulate themselves from suffering and discovery by believing a lie. Jesus learned obedience from suffering, but many will not allow this in their lives.

This "wisdom" is earthly. This means of the earth, of earthly wisdom and the earthly sphere or of the world's system, the harlot system. It is natural which means unspiritual.

This wisdom is demonic. This means that on the one hand this problem is unspiritual or natural. On the other hand, the wisdom is spiritual, just the wrong spirit. Demonic activity is always involved in this problem. Demons are just manifestations of the gods we serve. Or you could say the gods we serve have demons behind them. Both statements are valid.

We are idolaters at heart until God intervenes. We worship getting our own way. Demons influence our thoughts to help us do this. But as believers we must learn to put off these behaviors and not listen to the enemy's whispers.

James 3:17 "But the wisdom from above is first pure, then peaceable, gentle, reasonable, full of mercy and good fruits, unwavering, without hypocrisy. 18 And the seed whose fruit is righteousness is sown in peace by those who make peace." NASB

True wisdom is without hypocrisy, without masks. To the extent, a person is transparent they are approachable. Only the person who has laid aside the false identities and behavioral protections is a safe person. Only when we put these off can we truly put on the Lord Jesus Christ.

Eph. 4:20 "You, however, did not come to know Christ that way. 21 Surely you heard of him and were taught in him in accordance with the truth that is in Jesus. 22" You were taught, with regard to your former way of life, to put off your old self, which is being corrupted by its deceitful desires; 23 "to be made new in the attitude of your minds; 24 and to put on the new self, created to be like God in true righteousness and holiness."

First, we should put off our old self and falsehood. Second, we should put on the new self, *"created to be like God in true righteousness and holiness"*. We have at our disposal the indwelling presence of God to help us receive the transformation he purchased for us. We are to become more like God as his Spirit works within us transforming us. For this to happen we must commit to his will rather than our agenda, (business and field). We must commit to knowing him. Knowing him must become the over-riding passion of our life.

We must seek him in the word and speak the truth of his word against the lies that guide our lives. If we will allow knowledge of him to be our only passion and seek him in his word, we will put off those things that keep us from putting on our wedding garment.

Col. 3:6 "For it is because of these things that the wrath of God will come upon the sons of disobedience, 7" and in them you also once walked, when you were living in them. 8 "But now you also, put them all aside: anger, wrath, malice, slander, and abusive speech from your mouth. 9 "Do not lie to one another, since you laid aside the old self with its evil practices, 10 "and have put on the new self who is being renewed to a true knowledge according to the image of the One who created him — 11 "renewal in *which there is no distinction between Greek and Jew, circumcised and uncircumcised, barbarian, Scythian, slave and freeman, but **Christ is all, and in all.**"* (Emphasis mine) Christ is ALL, and He is in us helping us."

*Col. 3:12 "So, as those who have been chosen of God, holy and beloved, **put on a heart of compassion, kindness, humility, gentleness and patience;**"*

In Col. 3 we see we are to "put off the old self" and to put on not only the new self but a "heart of compassion, kindness, humility, gentleness and patience". We are to put on the new self in the Creator's image and put on the saint's righteous acts. So, putting off readies us to put on the new self and the righteous acts *(Rev. 19:8)* that make up the wedding garment. If we put off the old without putting on the new self, our efforts will fail. We must replace the lies with the truth to maintain freedom from the lies.

We can risk this and the suffering that goes with giving up everything we hold dear because we are beloved by him. In his eyes through his blood we are perfect. *Song 4:7 "You are all beautiful my darling and there is no flaw in you."* The Lord of All lives in us to empower us for the obedience he requires of us. He sees us as "all beautiful" and without flaw and he is Lord.

FOR REFLECTION

1. What should you put off from your life? How would God have you do this?

2. What should you put on in place of the lies? Write down how you will do this.

85

3. What will you change so you can come to know Christ intimately?

4. Will you commit to whatever it takes to get ready for the Bridegroom? Tell him your commitment and ask his help. Then listen and write what he says to you.

PRAYER

Lord there is much I need to remove. I know if you pulled back the veil I would see more. Help! Show me how to align my heart with yours. Help me put off the old self, the enemy's lies and put on all that you are.

Help me draw near to you and be willing for the suffering it will take to see the lies that guide my life. Since they are my identity, I know this will be painful, but you are with me. Help me not pull back from the process and mostly not pull back from you. You are my hope, my help and my only answer.

CHAPTER 10
THE WEDDING REHEARSAL

Heb. 12:1 "Therefore, since we have so great a cloud of witnesses surrounding us, let us also lay aside every encumbrance and the sin which so easily entangles us, and let us run with endurance the race that is set before us, 2 fixing our eyes on Jesus, the author and perfecter of faith, who for the joy set before Him endured the cross, despising the shame, and has sat down at the right hand of the throne of God."

Scripture encourages us to lay aside every encumbrance and fix our eyes on Jesus. This means quit rehearsing the lies that keep you from seeing who he is. Rehearse what the word says about him and his love for you. Rehearse the truth every time the lie surfaces. This is difficult because we seldom recognize the lies. However, if we fix our eyes on him, if we choose him again and again, in time we will recognize those lies for what they are. We will see him with more clarity.

If we rehearse the lies, sin will entangle us. But the same areas where before sin defeated us will yield to victory if we rehearse what the word of God says against every lie. We must listen to his voice in the secret place of his presence, so we may hear his personal love talk to us.

If we are to be ready, we must not only consider him who suffered, but we too must suffer. We are told that we can *"fellowship by sharing in His sufferings,"* Phil. 3:7-11. We must deny ourselves and take up our cross and follow him. *(Lu. 9:23)*. If we even want to save our life, we will lose it (*Lu. 9:24*). As we saw the desire to live life on our own terms will cause us to lose the life he has for us. So, in complying with these things above we will suffer. We cannot come to him on his terms without these things being fulfilled in us. It takes our cross to wrestle from us our desires for life on our terms, our fight against denying ourselves and our hatred for suffering.

We must learn to yield our whole life to him, but when we start out, we do not know what this means. He must reveal this to us. We often think we deny ourselves only to find out there is more to deny. When suffering comes, we need to learn to lean into it. Suffering presents the opportunity to fellowship with him intimately. Intimate fellowship produces His likeness in us.

For centuries, the Israelites served God and mixed the worship of other gods with their worship. This brought in child sacrifice and injustice of many sorts. Also included were licentious sexual practices since many of these other religions sanctioned temple prostitutes as a part of worship. God was calling his people to fidelity to Him alone, but they kept turning aside to other gods who allowed them to practice sin.

One day, when the blood-guilt of child sacrifice became too much, he allowed Babylon to invade and take the people of Israel not killed in the battle captive to Babylon. This happens to us as well.

When we do not understand surrender and

fidelity he warns us. If we do not listen to the warning, he allows us to be taken captive to Babylon metaphorically through difficult circumstances. (For the story of the Babylonian captivity refer to *2 Ki. 24-25, 2 Chr. 9-36, Lamentations, Jeremiah 20-46, Ezra and Nehemiah.*)

When we dwell in Babylon, we experience confusion. Like the Israelites who lost their land, temple, livelihood and family members we feel as if everything we believed in and the things that sustained us are gone. Often, we find ourselves bitter and angry with God. We do not realize we are in a place critical to our growth. In fact, Babylon is where God separates the true worshippers from the pretenders. Those who chose God while in Babylon were the true worshippers. Those who mixed the gods of Babylon with the worship of Jehovah were pretenders.

Ponder what this next scripture says about suffering.

Romans 8:18 "For I consider that the sufferings of this present time are not worthy to be compared with the glory that is to be revealed to us. 19 For the anxious longing of the creation waits eagerly for the revealing of the sons of God. 20 For the creation was subjected to futility, not willingly, but because of Him who subjected it, in hope 21 that the creation itself also will be set free from its slavery to corruption into the freedom of the glory of the children of God."

The Israelites had to quit worshipping other gods. And they needed to know they had futile behaviors that kept them from worshipping God alone. Their suffering in Babylon would bring forth obedience and therefore the Glory of God.

Our suffering sets us free from the things that keep us from reflecting his glory if we will allow it. God subjected the creation to futility (Babylon) because of God's hope to set us free from slavery to our futility gods to become at last his children completely surrendered.

So, suffering at the very deepest level possible is part of the training and preparation for the wedding. Fellowshipping in his sufferings is the main element of our wedding rehearsal. We do not suffer alone if we will allow him close during these times. As we suffer we can have intimate fellowship with him.

This next passage speaks of a time of restoration after great desolation. Captive in Babylon for 70 years because of their idolatry and spiritual adultery, God released the Israelites to go back to Israel. Isaiah prophesied their defeat by Babylon 80 years before their captivity. Isaiah perceived what was coming and prophesied Judah's destruction. Jeremiah prophesied and saw the destruction with his own eyes. Babylon took the Promised Land away from the people to whom it was promised. Those who still sought YHWH knew they had no one to blame but themselves. During this time in Babylon they received a promise.

Is. 49:15 "Can a woman forget her nursing child and have no compassion on the son of her womb? Even these may forget, but I will not forget you. 16 "Behold, I have inscribed you on the palms of My hands; Your walls are continually before Me.

17 "Your builders hurry; Your destroyers and devastators will depart from you. 18 "Lift up your eyes and look around; All of them gather together, they come to you. As I live," declares the LORD, "You will surely put on all of them as jewels and bind them on as a bride. 19 "For your waste and desolate places and your destroyed land — Surely now you will be too cramped for the inhabitants., And those who swallowed you will be far away.' 20 "The children of whom you were bereaved will yet say in your ears, 'The place is too cramped for me; Make room for me that I may live here.' 21 "Then you will say in your heart, 'Who has begotten these for me, Since I have been bereaved of my children And am barren, an exile and a wanderer? And who has reared these? Behold, I was left alone; From where did these come?'"

Those who longed for God while a captive in Babylon were familiar with this scripture. When the release came to return to Israel, they went as a bride with great joy. They waited on this day with anticipation.

Many more stayed in Babylon because like the people invited to the King's wedding banquet, they did not long for the things important to the King. In fact, they had adjusted to their new life. They did not long for God and for the land he had given them. Their eyes were fixed on other things. Babylon's gods had become theirs. We also can accept these other gods and worship them along with God Almighty.

God told those who left Babylon to re-inhabit Israel that their destroyers would leave, and the builders would come. They were to put on the builders as the jewels a bride puts on for her wedding. The people of Judah were captive 70 years They had many wounds and thus needed healing because of the punishment of their sin. But if they accept the call of God to return from Babylon, he would restore them as a bride. He was calling them to relationship rather than knowledge. We too need healing and restoration as a bride. We need intimacy to transform us.

Babylon is necessary, so we surrender the futile ways of life passed down from our forefathers. Then we must embrace the new life given by the Bridegroom Lamb. We can only know this life as we spend time with him in his presence and word. Like the Israelites before us we worship other gods. God in his mercy warns us through others and through his word. When we don't listen, we end up in Babylon. The word Babylon means confusion. When we come in to dark months and years and cannot find our way often we are in Babylon. This could be a prolonged winter season characterized by loss of hope.

When we like, the Israelites are in Babylon to prove our devotion, will we assimilate into this new location or will we learn to long for the one true God? Will we long for what we knew but can no longer see? Will we learn to fix our eyes on Jesus?

Our promise if we come out of exile is bridal intimacy and spiritual children. These are the two promises that come out of two greatest commandments to love God with all our being and love our neighbors. Bridal intimacy will bring us into total love for God. Without Babylon, we may never be free enough to experience this.

For Reflection

1. Are you in a confusing time? Do you feel as if you are in Babylon? Pray for the Lord to help you understand where he is in this for you.

2. Will you allow him to be your comfort during this time.? Will you allow yourself to fellowship with him around the sufferings of Christ?

3. Let him show you what caused your exile. Write them down and pray through them and listen in his presence and word for the antidote to them.

4. Continue to pray over the weeks, months and years so he can continue to reveal other things that keep you from bridal intimacy. Remember he promises you will put on your bridal jewelry and have sons and daughters.

PRAYER

Lord forgive me for the things I worship along with you that I cannot yet see. I want to worship only you. Set me free from the futility of my idolatry.

Help me to seek you amid suffering rather than running from you. Bring me into bridal intimacy. You are my overriding hope.

CHAPTER 11
CITY OF WARRIORS-MORE REHEARSAL

Those who walk in intimacy find many challenges in their lives and many obstacles to overcome. In fact, the scripture is clear in *Romans 8*. God subjects us to futility, so he might set us free from our tendency toward sin into the freedom of the children of God. This means we will fight many spiritual battles. Some of these battles are futile; we sense that nothing we try works. This is because we trust in other gods, other behaviors not compatible with our life in God.

The book that carries more information than any other about the many positive attributes we possess in God's sight is Song of Songs. In this book, we read:

Song 4:4 "Your neck is like the tower of David, built with elegance; on it hang a thousand shields, all of them shields of warriors."

The tower of David is a watchtower with shields of war hanging on it. These shields are small shields each soldier used in close combat. This has several applications. The first application is that she is a watchtower watching for the enemy's approach. She sees the enemy coming and can warn others. The second application is that the ornaments she is wearing on her neck are shields with which to engage in hand-to-hand combat. She has many shields. These are shields for those she will mentor so the might enter in to warfare.

These are the shield of faith in the book of Ephesians. The Lord sees her calling to warfare and knows her faith will sustain her in her calling. There are battles to win for our King of Love. She does not know the fullness of this yet, but he sees it as he looks at her. This is the Lord's first mention of her as a warrior. Others follow.

Song 6:4 "You are beautiful, my darling, as Tirzah, lovely as Jerusalem, majestic as troops with banners."

The word Tirzah means delightsome. Tirzah was a city in the northern kingdom of Israel. This city was so beautiful its name was delightsome. Tirzah was set on a hill. Cities set on hills have an advantage in times of warfare.

Matthew 5:14 "You are the light of the world. A city on a hill cannot be hidden.

Not only is she a city with a warfare advantage, Matthew tells us she is a light. When she wins battles for the King, the light that comes from her city draws others to her, so they can discover the secret of her power and her light. Because of her power and light the following takes place.

"The Friends say:
Song 6:10 'Who is this that grows like the dawn,
As beautiful as the full moon,
As pure as the sun,
As awesome as an army with banners?'"

This bride has dawning, gradual light as she is viewed by others. Her beauty is like moonlight at its fullest. Her purity is like the brightest light. Sunlight sustains that which it impacts. And she is an awesome army volunteer. So awesome that she looks like an entire army this is because she is. She has mentored others, and they have joined her in the Kings battles.

The banner of the King puts fear into the hearts of the adversary. Those around the bride see her power and her light. Even the light of the sun generates power and causes the power of nature to produce the things we need to live. However, the power they see in this bride of the Lord is so vast it resembles an army with many banners. It is one thing to have the Lord recognize her power by describing her as an army with banners, and another thing for others to recognize it. This means they recognize the source of the power.

She is an army. She knows how to engage in warfare and how to yield to the power of the King. His power is displayed on the banners and He gives the power to her to wield on his behalf until he comes again to make all kingdoms his. Further, she is to occupy until he comes. This means win territory and keep it, do not let the enemy have it back. She has the power for this with his power at work within her.

To be a warrior requires great discipline and obedience. One does not get to choose which orders one obeys. Military discipline requires instant obedience to every order. When we understand the warfare, the bride engages in, the need for obedience to the commands of the King becomes more important. She must know the heart of the King for a strategy to defeat the enemy. The King can see things she cannot, and she must know the correct move to take to stop the enemy in his nefarious schemes. In fact, people's lives depend on it.

The bride as a warrior underscores the importance prayer plays in the life of the church. Prayer is not only making requests. It is also listening for a strategy, for the next step. It is pouring our hearts out to God about everything and listening for him to pour his heart out to us.

Somewhere in the worship/prayer exchange he shows us how to triumph. First, we must learn for our own lives and then for the lives of others. She has shields enough for herself and to help train others. She is a city on a hill with battle advantage and the light of God within her.

Song 6:12. "Before I was aware, my soul set me over the chariots of my noble people."

Here we see chariots. Before the bride could think, she found herself over the chariots of God's people. She has shields and chariots at her disposal, so she might be successful in warfare. The bride has battle strategy because she listens in the secret place. She can lead the chariots, the warriors because she knows the next moves of the King.

Song 6:13 "Come back, come back, O Shulammite; Come back, come back, that we may gaze at you!" "Why should you gaze at the Shulammite, as on the dance of Mahanaim?"

In the first part of the verse the friends ask Shulammite to come back so they may gaze at her.

They want to see her because when they see her they view the love and devotion and glory of the Bridegroom Lamb. Christ shown forth in the life of the believer is often how others come to desire him. She has been involved in warfare with the chariots, but now the friends ask for her, so they might grow in the things she has perfected.

The next part of the verse is the Bridegroom speaking. *"Why would you gaze on the bride as on the dance of Mahanaim?"*

The root word for Mahanaim means an encampment, an army of dancers, soldiers etc. [xi] This refers to *Genesis 32:1-2 "Jacob also went on his way and the angels of God met him. When Jacob saw them he said, 'This is the camp of God!' So he named that place Mahanaim."* Jacob was traveling to see Esau. Along the way heavenly troops met Jacob's army, and they formed one army.

The bride is not alone in her battles. This is an army of volunteers like her, willing to give all to know him, and the angels of God fight with this army.

This verse shows her as a warrior who dances as a part of her warfare. She is the warrior dancer bride.

The Dancer

Once men would say
dance dancer dance.
She danced and served
and served and danced.

Joy was not in the dance,
not in the slave's dance.

Now she is set free
to dance for the King,
Set free from hard servitude.
Dance dancer dance.
Dance with joy,
the joy of the bride.
not the obligation of the slave.

Dance dancer dance
There are victories to be won
for the King of love.

Dance dancer dance.
Listen to the great choreographer
and dance the dance
He has written for you
No other dance will do.

As you dance before His love banner
the enemy is pushed back.
he cannot withstand your beauty.
he cannot overcome your joy.
he cannot stop your love.

Your feet dance on the high places
of the earth.
You scale the places that
other feet cannot go.
You are being watched by those
who cannot believe you would be so loved.

They want to know
that what you know
is possible.

So, dance dancer dance
 and win for your Love
the desire of His heart.
The company of dancers in the
Earth that shine like the sun.

These people see him and love him. Their
hearts sing, *"I belong to my lover, and his desire is for
me."* They know the love of the Bridegroom in its
truth and glory. They are a force in the earth. Every
church age has known this people. Today, the Lord
saved the best wine for last, so it is true more so.
The day we live in demands it.

This description is of the dancer he died to
purchase. He invites us to be that dancer. Have you
accepted the invitation? Will you accept it now?

Hear the rejoicing over the harlot's
judgement and the readiness of the bride:

*Rev. 19:1 "After these things I heard
something like a loud voice of a great multitude in
heaven, saying, 'Hallelujah! salvation and glory and
power belong to our God;*

*Rev. 19:2 'BECAUSE HIS JUDGMENTS ARE
TRUE AND RIGHTEOUS; for He has judged the great
harlot who was corrupting the earth with her
immorality, and HE HAS AVENGED THE BLOOD OF
HIS BOND-SERVANTS ON HER.'" Rev. 19:3 'And a
second time they said, "Hallelujah! HER SMOKE
RISES UP FOREVER AND EVER.'*

Rev. 19:4 "And the twenty-four elders and the four living creatures fell down and worshiped God who sits on the throne saying, 'Amen. Hallelujah!'

Rev. 19:5 "And a voice came from the throne, saying, 'Give praise to our God, all you His bond-servants, you who fear Him, the small and the great.'

Rev. 19:6 "Then I heard something like the voice of a great multitude and like the sound of many waters and like the sound of mighty peals of thunder, saying, 'Hallelujah! For the Lord our God, the Almighty, reigns.

Rev. 19:7 'Let us rejoice and be glad and give the glory to Him, for the marriage of the Lamb has come and His bride has made herself ready.

Rev. 19:8 'It was given to her to clothe herself in fine linen, bright and clean; for the fine linen is the righteous acts of the saints.'

Rev. 19:9 "Then he said to me, Write, 'Blessed are those who are invited to the marriage supper of the Lamb.'" "And he said to me, "These are true words of God."'

There is a bride in the earth that "made herself ready". She is obedient and as a result she has received her garments from the King. She learns to dance the army dance. Because of her many have joined the bride company. Because of her the harlot is ultimately judged. She is in the company of the dancers of Mahanaim.

The two armies, the army of God and the bride company are as one. No longer does she wonder how to draw near to her Lover because she walks near to him all the time. Her every movement is under his direction. They dance, he leads, and she follows. See her dance in the earth with him at the lead.

FOR REFLECTION

1. Are you ready to know the strategy of God to overcome the plan of the enemy in your life? How about the lives of others, in your city, in our nation?
2. Will you commit to fight and engage in warfare for the things that matter to God?
3. Will you allow your heart to become so one with his that when he takes a step you follow? Will you dance in the earth with him at the lead?

PRAYER

Lord I want to be the warrior dancer bride. Teach me the steps of obedience so I may dance your dance. Teach me how to press in not only for battle strategy, but so I may hear your voice in the Secret Place of your presence. *"Your voice is sweet, and your form is lovely."*

Lord I want to follow your every step and dance victories for you my King of Love.

CHAPTER 12

THE READY BRIDE

Ps. 45 states this about our King in verse *9,* *"At Your right hand stands the queen in gold from Ophir."* This bride is his people, clothed with the garments he provides.   Solomon used the gold of Ophir[xii] in armor, his throne, his house and the temple. Ophir was "the" source of gold in Solomon's day. The bride is wearing gold of Ophir. The King provides her adornment.

Then it speaks to us. *Psa. 45:10 "Listen, O daughter, give attention and incline your ear: Forget your people and your father's house;"* To be ready, we, like this bride must forget the futile way of life handed down to us from our forefathers. Since our futile way of life is the only way we know to behave, this directive is difficult. How can we find strength and enlightenment we need to continue to leave behind these ways?

11 "Then the King will desire your beauty. Because He is your Lord, bow down to Him." There are two things we need to know.   First, he is enthralled with us as we submit to him and receive from him the eye salve, white garments and gold he provides. (Rev. 3) His smitten heart will sustain us if we will seek him out. He wants us to be much in his presence for his heart desires us. The second thing, is we honor him in this seeking and through this we declare His Lordship over all we are. We bow to him. Through submission we will find enlightenment about our "stuff". Humility will enable us to hear his voice, and his voice and word bring freedom. Maturity arrives when we forget our father's house.

12 "The daughter of Tyre will come with a gift; The rich among the people will seek your favor." As the result of this total trust and submission he gives bride a place of influence with others. Others bring gifts to her.

13 "The King's daughter is all glorious within; Her clothing is interwoven with gold. 14 She will be led to the King in embroidered work; The virgins, her companions who follow her, will be brought to You."

He provides the garment, but she must wear it. Song of Songs contains a passage that describes her as he saw her when he died. There is much more to the passage as far as his description of her than in the poem below, but the poem below captures their wedding day as present in Song of Songs. Notice the contrast between her beauty and his. Picture their wedding day.

Wedding Song

The bride glorious in holiness
meets the King,
myrrh, frankincense and cassia her
sweet perfumes.

Garments white, interwoven

with gold adorn her,
and a jeweled crown is on her head.

The Bridegroom covered in
redemption meets the bride,
He is the incense on the altar
before the throne.
Naked He hangs between
earth and heaven,
and thorns bejewel the crown
upon His head.

His love poured forth on this
Their wedding day,
as He stood intercessor
between God and man.
The richness of His blood
has washed her clean,
and now holy, she comes
unto the Lamb.

Receive this Secret Place truth. Remove the veils that separate you from Him. You are his.

2 Cor. 3:18 "But we all, with unveiled face, beholding as in a mirror the glory of the Lord, are being transformed into the same image from glory to glory, just as from the Lord, the Spirit."

Rev 19:7 "Let us rejoice and be glad and give the glory to Him, for the marriage of the Lamb has come and His bride has made herself ready."

FOR REFLECTION:

1. By searching the scriptures in this book and other scriptures that relate to the content what can you do to realize change? Let the Lord show you the answers he desires in your life.

2. What areas of your attitude and beliefs are in error? What other gods do you serve? Do you fear rejection, poverty, exposure of your defectiveness, uncovering of your shame or sin? Do you give yourself to your electronics rather than the Lord? Write down the other gods. What scriptures can you memorize (keep) to change your incorrect beliefs?

3. Do you believe you must perform to receive love? What does God say about His love for you? How can these truths help you? Record the things he is speaking to you. Then visit these truths until they are so a part of you that the enemy can no longer lie to you and say you are not loved or that you must perform to be loved. Ref. Song 4:7, E Cor. 3:18, Ps.17:15, Phil. 3:7-8.

4. Ask the Lord to show you the place in his heart to which he calls you. Write what he says and make this the trajectory of your heart.

PRAYER

Dear Bridegroom Lamb, I did not know my heart could still be so askew. I thought it was yours, but I see that is only partly true. Draw me and bring me into your presence even if I resist. Show me the many gods I serve that keep me from seeing you. Help me to focus on you.

Forgive me my King for my inability or unwillingness to see. I am blind but did not know it. I have been wretched and thought it was normal. I am impoverished and thought I was rich. I am deceived and believed I was following truth. Today I ask to buy from you gold refined in your fire and white clothing to cover my nakedness, and eye salve so I might see.

Whatever the price of these things I give you permission to receive that price from my life. I ask only that you will help me to understand in a new way that you are with me and you desire me above all else. May you fill my vision and your presence fill my heart every moment, so I will want no one and nothing but you.

CHAPTER 13
THE GLORIOUS BRIDE

What follows describes the Lord's glorious bride. We will investigate this to understand how we may be ready. In fact, this description is of the one who has been the eternal object of His affections.

Rev. 21:9 "Then one of the seven angels who had the seven-bowls full of the seven last plagues came and spoke with me, saying, 'Come here, I will show you the bride, the wife of the Lamb.' 10 And he carried me away in the Spirit to a great and high mountain, and showed me the holy city, Jerusalem, coming down out of heaven from God, 11 having the glory of God. Her brilliance was like a very costly stone, as a stone of crystal-clear jasper. 12 It had a great and high wall, with twelve gates, and at the gates twelve angels; and names were written on them, which are the names of the twelve tribes of the sons of Israel. 13 There were three gates on the east and three gates on the north and three gates on the south and three gates on the west. 14 And the wall of the city had twelve foundation stones, and on them were the twelve names of the twelve apostles of the Lamb."

It is significant that one angel who came to judge the harlot Babylon introduces the bride. Each of us that is part of the bride performs assigned tasks in obedience to the King much like the angel that took part in the Harlot's judgment. Even when we find the task negative or difficult, we must fulfill it.

Since the angels in heaven rejoice over one repentant sinner one can only imagine how the angels must have watched for the end of the Harlot. They know now the desire of the Bridegroom's heart; that the bride can come forth in the glory she has received from Him. The angels know he is worthy, and they have waited for this culmination.

Not only is she introduced as his bride; scripture calls her the wife of the Lamb. She is now his eternal spouse and will live in intimate heart to heart relationship with him eternally.

Then the angel presents her as a city shining with the glory of God. She has twelve gates, three on each side with the names of the twelve tribes of Israel and twelve foundations with the names of the apostles of the Lamb.

This city comprises true believers from all times. The Apostles laid the foundation, so the city could be built upon it. Until the Lamb came and died, no one understood the Old Testament prophecies well. It was in the Lamb's sacrifice that the past and his great love could be understood.

This city could not be complete without the twelve tribes of Israel, those who believed in Old Testament times and the 12 Apostles of the Lamb. Belief in every age includes obedience and intimacy.

Rev. 21:15 "The one who spoke with me had a gold measuring rod to measure the city, and its gates and its wall. 16 The city is laid out as a square, and its length is as great as the width; and he measured the city with the rod, fifteen hundred miles; its length and width and height are equal. 17 And he measured its wall, seventy-two yards, according to human measurements, which are also angelic measurements. 18 The material of the wall was jasper; and the city was pure gold, like clear glass. 19 The foundation stones of the city wall were adorned "with every kind of precious stone. The first foundation stone was jasper; the second, sapphire; the third, chalcedony; the fourth, emerald; 20 the fifth, sardonyx; the sixth, sardius; the seventh, chrysolite; the eighth, beryl; the ninth, topaz; the tenth, chrysoprase; the eleventh, jacinth; the twelfth, amethyst. 21 And the twelve gates were twelve pearls; each one of the gates was a single pearl. And the street of the city was pure gold, like transparent glass."

The angel measured the city. It was 1500 miles high, wide and long. It is a foursquare city, a glorious vast city. This is the shape of the Temple's Holy of Holies. It was a perfect cube. This city is the real. The Holy of Holies in the Temple was a type. This city was in God's heart from times beginning. Everything that occurred in history was to culminate in the bringing forth of this city, the eternal dwelling of the people of God, his bride.

Those who hunger for the intimacy he calls us to as his bride know the temple and the Holy of Holies help them understand how to enter God's presence. Their heart's cry goes something like this:

The Secret Place

Lamp-stand, showbread, only types of Him
Into whose presence, I must now come.

Not trusting the ritual of the stand and bread.
But looking unto Him in that Secret Place.

Putting aside all types and shadows,
facsimiles and caricatures of Him.

What my mind thinks will not suffice.
My eye must behold Him in the Secret Place.

Then I will know who He really is.
Not just what men would say
or types and shadows show.

Then will I learn to be content
 in Him
only in Him.

The walls are pure gold, the foundations are 12 different precious stones and the twelve gates are 12 pearls. This contrasts with cities of ancient days with dirt streets, stonewalls and open sewers. The pearl gates speak of purity. The streets of this city are pure gold like transparent glass. This gold is beyond the pure gold of our day. Though we could see our reflection in pure gold, we cannot see through it as if transparent. The purity of this city is beyond comprehension just as the holiness of God is unfathomable.

Rev. 21:22 "I saw no temple in it, for the Lord God the Almighty and the Lamb are its temple. 23 And the city has no need of the sun or of the moon to shine on it, for the glory of God has illumined it, and its lamp is the Lamb. 24 The nations will walk by its light, and the kings of the earth will bring their glory into it. 25 n the daytime (for there will be no night there) its gates will never be closed; 26 and they will bring the glory and the honor of the nations into it; 27 and nothing unclean, and no one who practices abomination and lying, shall ever come into it, but only those whose names are written in the Lamb's book of life."

This city needs no sun or moon or light of any kind. Like the Holy of Holies, the glory of God gives it light, and the Lamb is its lamp. The bride is preparing even now as she spends time with God in the Secret Place, the Holy of Holies of his presence. In fact, she is giving of her time and her life allowing him to change her until she is transformed by his glory. Then she ministers to others out of that place and they also desire him. They want him because they view his glory in her. Nothing unclean will enter this city and only those whose names are written in the Lamb's book will inhabit it.

Rev. 22:1 "Then he showed me a river of the water of life, clear as crystal, coming from the throne of God and of the Lamb, 2 in the middle of its street On either side of the river was the tree of life, bearing twelve kinds of fruit, yielding its fruit every month;

and the leaves of the tree were for the healing of the nations. 3 There will no longer be any curse; and the throne of God and of the Lamb will be in it, and His bond-servants will serve Him; 4 they will see His face, and His name will be on their foreheads. 5 And there will no longer be any night; and they will not have need of the light of a lamp nor the light of the sun, because the Lord God will illumine them; and they will reign forever and ever".

Next, we see a river of the water of life and the tree of life yielding year-round fruit. No more will the tree of knowledge defile humanity. No more will we struggle with the sin nature. God broke the curse for eternity. God's throne is present. He will rule forever.

The bride's yearning to see His face is fulfilled eternally. The bride rules and reigns with her Holy Husband forever and ever.

Bride City of God

The King reigns and
His glory shines
from the city of His heart.

The focal point of heaven
is this city.
His throne dwells there.
His light illuminates every corner.
The emerald rainbow lights her.
The sea of glass illumines her.
Glory shines from her,
refined as pure gold,

purified as transparent gold,
the King her only light.
She carries His heart
forever.
She always has.
From before time began
she was His,
forever His.

History ends, and eternity begins. Are you willing to make yourself ready? "The Spirit and the bride say come." The Bridegroom awaits.

Bibliography

[ii] Strong's Greek Dictionary of the New Testament (Greek Strong's), Public Domain

[iii] The Ryrie Study Bible — Expanded Edition, by Charles Caldwell Ryrie., © 1986 & 1995 by The Moody Bible Institute of Chicago.

[iv] Unger's Bible Dictionary, The New Unger's Bible Dictionary   (Unger's Dictionary), by Merrill F. Unger, R. K. Harrison, editor, Used by permission of Moody Bible Institute of Chicago, All rights reserved.

[v] Ibid Strong's

[vi] Macarthur's Bible Commentary Copyright 1985-2009, Moody Bible Institute

[vii] Unger's Bible Dictionary

[viii] Smiths's Bible Dictionary, 1889, Public Domain

[ix] Ungers

[x] Strong's
[xi] Strong's Hebrew Chaldee Dictionary of Old Testament Words, Public Domain

Made in United States
Troutdale, OR
07/20/2023

11427854R00072